THE ETHER DOME

Also by Allen Grossman

P O E T R Y

The Song of the Lord. An audio tape on which the author reads poems selected
from *The Ether Dome,* published by Watershed Tapes.

A Harlot's Hire (1961)

The Recluse (1965)

And the Dew Lay All Night Upon My Branch (1973)

The Woman on the Bridge Over the Chicago River (1979)

Of the Great House: A Book of Poems (1982)

The Bright Nails Scattered on the Ground (1986)

P R O S E

Poetic Knowledge in the Early Yeats (1970)

The Sighted Singer: Two Works on Poetry for Readers and Writers, with Mark
Halliday (1991). Revised and augmented edition containing *Against Our
Vanishing: Winter and Summer Conversations on the Theory and Practice of Poetry*
(1980, 1990), and *Summa Lyrica: A Primer of the Commonplaces in Speculative
Poetics* (The Johns Hopkins University Press).

ALLEN GROSSMAN

THE ETHER DOME
and Other Poems

NEW AND SELECTED

(1 9 7 9 – 1 9 9 1)

A NEW DIRECTIONS BOOK

Grateful acknowledgment is made to the editors of magazines in which some of the poems in the first section of this volume previously appeared: *Agni, Boulevard, Erato: Harvard Book Review, New Directions 54, Ploughshares, Tikkun, Western Humanities Review.* "Poland of Death (I)" and "Poland of Death (II)" were reprinted in *Pushcart Prize XII: Best of the Small Presses 1987–1988* (Pushcart Press). "The Piano Player Explains Himself" was included in *Best American Poetry 1988* (Macmillan), edited by John Ashbery and David Lehman and "The Ether Dome" in *Best American Poetry 1990,* edited by Mark Strand and David Lehman (Macmillan).

The poems in sections II, III, and IV were first collected in the following books by Allen Grossman: *The Woman on the Bridge over the Chicago River* (Copyright © 1974, 1977, 1978, 1979 by Allen Grossman), New Directions; *Of the Great House* (Copyright © 1980, 1981, 1982, by Allen Grossman), New Directions; *The Bright Nails Scattered on the Ground* (Copyright © 1984, 1985, 1986 by Allen Grossman), New Directions.

Manufactured in the United States of America
New Directions Books are printed on acid-free paper.
First published clothbound and as New Directions Paperbook 723 in 1991
Published simultaneously in Canada by Penguin Books Canada Limited

Library of Congress Cataloging in Publication Data

Grossman, Allen R., 1932–
    The ether dome and other poems : new and selected (1979–1991) / Allen
Grossman
        p.   cm.
    ISBN 0–8112–1184–3. — ISBN 0–8112–1179–7 (pbk.)
        I. Title.
    PS3557.R67E8   1991
    811'.54—dc20   91–13845
                                                                           CIP

New Directions Books are published for James Laughlin
by New Directions Publishing Corporation,
80 Eighth Avenue, New York 10011

Contents

I. *Pastorals of Our Other Hours in the Millennium*   1

The Piano Player Explains Himself   3
The Life and Death Kisses   5
The Ether Dome   7
    1. O wondrous universe!   7
    2. I fell in love.   8
    3. What do I love?   9
    4. Someone lies on a path.   10
    5. By such a light as this.   11
    6. Where is the sun today?   12
    7. Above the pages.   13
    8. All things visible and invisible.   14
    9. A fulgurous flash!   16
    10. "You must know everything."   17
A Pastoral   19
Flax   21
A Summer Day   24
Mary Snorak the Cook, Skermo the Gardener, and Jack
the Parts Man Provide Dinner for a Wandering Stranger   26
Spring Song of the Behemoth   28
Poland of Death   30
    I. "I hear my father underground"   30
    II. "As not in life my father appeared to me"   31
    III. "The dead are beyond caring."   33
    IV. "It is the duty of every man"   35
    V. "There are many waves"   40
Mrs. O'Leary's Cat   43
Out of the Blue   45
Phoenix   50
A Music Lesson   53
Dust   56

II. from *The Woman on the Bridge over the Chicago River* (1979) 59

The Woman on the Bridge over the Chicago River   61
The Room   63
The Book of Father Dust   64
By the Pool   67
The Runner   68
The Field, Her Pleasure   69
A Snowy Walk   71
Pat's Poem   73
Two Waters   75
The Loss of the Beloved Companion   76
After Repetition   79
The Ballad of the Bone Boat   81
O Great O North Cloud   83
Nightmare   84
The Lady of Villa Malcontenta Departs with the Dawn Light   85
The Thrush Relinquished   87
Victory   88
The Department   91
Lament Fragment   95
The Lecture   97

III. from *Of the Great House* (1982)   99

Of the Great House   101
    I. To the poets   101
    II. The dream of rescue   104
    III. The throat of the hourglass   106
    IV. At the shore   108
    V. The only thing that is   110
The Slave   113
Bow Spirit   118
A Little Sleep   126
The Prothanation of a Charioteer   131
Sentinel Yellowwoods   138
An Inventory of Destructions   141

IV. from *The Bright Nails Scattered on the Ground* (1986)   147

    The Song of the Lord   149
    The Work   150
    The Gate   151
    A Short Walk   153
    At the Shore   155
    The Patience of the Darker Lover   156
    The Stare   157
    The Lock   158
    Eurydice, or the Third Reich of Dreams   160
    The Jew's Daughter   166
    To the Trumpets   168
    Stanzas on the Mourning of Nativity   170
    The Broom   174
    The Path   176
    The Guardian   177
    The Sound of a Voice is the Story of Itself   178
    Quies, or Rest   180

I

*Pastorals
of Our Other Hours
in the Millennium*

THE PIANO PLAYER EXPLAINS HIMSELF

When the corpse revived at the funeral,
The outraged mourners killed it; and the soul
Of the revenant passed into the body
Of the poet because it had more to say.
He sat down at the piano no one could play
Called Messiah, or The Regulator of the World,
Which had stood for fifty years, to my knowledge,
Beneath a painting of a red-haired woman
In a loose gown with one bared breast, and played
A posthumous work of the composer S——
About the impotence of God (I believe)
Who has no power not to create everything.
It was the Autumn of the year and wet,
When the music started. The musician was
Skillful but the Messiah was out of tune
And bent the time and the tone. For a long hour
The poet played The Regulator of the World
As the spirit prompted, and entered upon
The pathways of His power—while the mourners
Stood with slow blood on their hands
Astonished by the weird processional
And the undertaker figured his bill.
—We have in mind an unplayed instrument
Which stands apart in a memorial air
Where the room darkens toward its inmost wall
And a lady hangs in her autumnal hair
At evening of the November rains; and winds
Sublime out of the North, and North by West,
Are sowing from the death-sack of the seed
The burden of her cloudy hip. Behold,
I send the demon I know to relieve your need,
An imperfect player at the perfect instrument
Who takes in hand The Regulator of the World

To keep the splendor from destroying us.
Lady! The last virtuoso of the composer S——
Darkens your parlor with the music of the Law.
When I was green and blossomed in the Spring
I was mute wood. Now I am dead I sing.

THE LIFE AND DEATH KISSES

ibant obscuri

The chroniclers ceased, they ceased . . . until I arose—
Out of the infinite unborn, one of the born who lived,
And out of the number of all who have lived and died,
One of those yet alive,
And among all who are yet alive, one of us not in the greatest
Pain, not demented, not buried and awaiting rescue without hope
Under a cruel weight, and not mourning inconsolable losses
Night after night, or enraged by the treachery of women,
Or subjected (not for *this moment,* thank God!) by the evil
Power of J—

Arose, in truth, because it was time, punctually,
At three in the afternoon, from where I was sitting without
Thought on an obdurate bright bench of varnished rattan
In the last car of a train—leaning and slowing as on a curve—
Beside a honey-blond woman of indeterminate age whose
Eyes were strange—
Amidst the blandness of air and the thin light of destination.
It was in the middle-western state of X— Land of Lakes—,
Somewhere on the western, unbuilt limb of the central city
Where lordly factories, and highways, and nursing homes were
Transparent with hesitation between then and now in sunlight
Whiter than it should be

Because the foul windows of the old train were crowded with
Papery faces—like bleached leaves fallen to the bottom of
An empty pool, one upon the other; or like ocean waves blown down
White by the silent hurricane, waves breaking out of sight of land,
Unsurvivable by ships—
Human beings with the faces of leaves or fallen water:
Near at hand the faces that *can* appear, and behind them also
The ones that *cannot* appear, in their multitudes, white faces

Receding into the whiteness of the light and the flat landscape
Of the Great Plains of the dream.

I rose to get down, for the train had stopped and it was
Leaning in the light. And I looked on my right hand to the woman
Who sat beside me—the stout, blond woman with strange eyes—,
Thinking, "She will know the way. This is her country."
But I saw she was blind.
She was blind. I knew by the hesitation of her body as she
Lifted it like something very large with separate intentions
In another world. She took hold of me and we entered the dark end
Of the car, and then she kissed me with life and death kisses
Amid a great rush of air mingled with odors of metal,
And the slamming of doors. And out of her mouth a stone passed
Into my open mouth.

"This is the stone of witness," she said, "that stops every heart."
Thereafter, I turned to the left hand and went down. In the sunlight
A Spring snow was rising and falling on the plain, and the rails
Where the train had been
Were brimming with silver. I would have lingered in the light
For the interest of the empty scene, but I was wearied out
By the silence of life and death, and the kisses of the Fate.
And I lay down among the leaves like a young soul bewildered,
Beneath a sun that was as a stare of the finest eye. And then,
The life stopped in me, and the witness-stone divided my throat.

THE ETHER DOME

(An Entertainment)

"I'm going to foreign parts, brother."
"Foreign parts?"
"To America."
"America?"
Svidrigaylov took out a revolver and cocked it.
Achilles raised his eyebrow.
"Vot now, this is not the place for jokes!"
"Why shouldn't it be the place?"
"Because it isn't."
"Well, brother, it doesn't matter. It's a good place . . .
If you are asked, say I said I was off to America."
He lifted the revolver to his right temple.

Crime and Punishment

1.   O wondrous universe!

O wondrous universe! O beautiful one!
Never more ocean, the work of God,
Nor nepenthe, nor mandragora, nor vapors of hemp!
Never more the moon, a man of stone,
Never more earth, pastor of the dead!
And the sun—that clumsy arsonist—has fled
The burning factories of the dawn
(A double agent with an absolute device,
Ambiguous instructions and a suspicious limp)
Who was at noon, according to police reports,
Far to the south—out of this ice. —But you
And I are growing old. . . . It is Autumn
In America. And there is a body
On the path in the Public Garden.

Someone

Has stopped to think beneath a monument,

As if it were the last chance of the mind
Before the Millennium. Thus, at the end of life,
The philosophers of pain must bid, "Farewell!"
To all the countries of the world with their dying breath,
Or *in extremis* sigh: "What has been concluded
That we may conclude with regard to it?"—
Unless a poet tells the story ("Let us begin!").
Then, they all sit down beside their shadows on
The ground, like weary shepherds in a pastoral.
"Tell us," they insist, "what happened to *you?*"
And for a moment, "Farewell!" hangs like a moon
Not yet risen below the horizon
Of all the countries of the world—until
The song and the echoes of the song are done.

2. I fell in love.

I fell in love with a woman at a party,
In Cambridge Massachusetts, thirty years ago.
It was one of the other hours, and one
Of the other loves—when Love has something in mind
She will not suffer us not to know. Therefore,
In a room to which I never can return,
Suddenly I saw the Lady of Pain
Who rules the Ether Dome. Her name is Asenath,
As full of memories as wind and rain.
She had grey eyes, and appeared to be surrounded
By children and animals. I knew from the start
She was a woman who preferred to live near water.
"How does it feel to be the beautiful one?"
I thought, "Is it a kind of happiness?" But she said,
"Come!" Then I followed the children and animals
Under the blue firmament of the Ether Dome,
Her kingdom. She showed me a table there laid out
In knives—a table, and a bed. To the left,
A god in plaster, Apollo Belvedere, expressing ease.

To the right, an Egyptian mummy with uncovered eyes,
Black hair, and her teeth still in her head.
On the bed lay the body of a man, or a woman,
A *body* in any case—the sad Miami of a soul:
Suffering and death in a beautiful place
Near water, unconscious, subject to the Law.
Two men in aprons worked with bloody knives
At a prominent cyst in the lower jaw.
Both wore dark suits, and shirts laundered in France.
There was an odor in the air like moly crushed
Or the oblivion of a long romance:
"Here first," she said, "under this azure dome
Anaesthesia was devised (by ether in a sponge)
Producing insensibility to pain.
Knowledge of that discovery spread from
This room to all the countries of the world,
And a new era for surgery began. . . ."
Her voice, memorious as wind and rain.

3. What do I love?

Philosophers of pain, what do I love?
What does love *intend* by this mysterious
Pastoral that prolongs "Farewell!", and adorns
The end of a grave thought with the carnality of rhyme:
Apollo of the charming scrotum, his arrow gone elsewhere;
An everlasting mummy with vanity of teeth and hair;
Two men in black with knives mending a jaw;
An odor in the air, uncanny, arousing awe?
I loved the traffic of the waters in her voice,
The great whales in it, the weeds and horns,
The children on her bosom—like infants at the shore
Of a warm sea. Love wanted me to know
The lady of pain in the time of the other hours,
The beautiful one with storm-grey eyes, the blind
Pastor of animals in the Millennium
(*Nostra effige*), who said to me, "Be true

To the poet's word! Work hard! Restore the gods!
And die in your time. This is my tomb. Love
Intends another odor and another room
In which the human image dwells serene
Among the things of stone—witness to the universe—
The greatest poet—flesh and bone—(she paused)—
And send your shirts to France if you want them clean."

4. Someone lies on a path.

Someone lies on a path in the Public Garden
(The dream-body moves, the real is still
And makes no motion), drunk or lost in sleep
Beneath a monument without a name—the last
Chance of the mind before the Millennium.
The heavy engine of the unseen moon
Hammers at the sill of night—"Farewell!", "Farewell!"—
Like a freight train on a grade, running late,
Raising up the cold stone of the moon's light
Above the horizon of all the countries of the world.
The paths of the Public Garden are chill and dry.
The philosophers of pain are dead, their shadows gone.
The song and the echoes of the song are done.
Far off a woman or a man, with jaw intact,
Is barking like a dog at the dilation
Of the lunar dawn—the petition of a nation!
—And Apollo descends on America
Out of a barren mountain of the moon
(A pinnacle, in fact, of fiery snow).
Terrible is the bang of the arrows in his quiver,
Terrible is the twang of his silver bow:
The one arrow of age with a ragged edge
That cannot be withdrawn, and a second arrow,
Tipped with the leaf of the elm, the aspen, or the beech
(No metal harder) that flies with a cry,
Like the sparrow, of the sorrow of children;
And another arrow which is sorrow

For the children's sorrow. In the shadows of ships
I saw Apollo kneel on the moon-grey sedge,
Among the mice at the Atlantic shore, and shower
Arrow after arrow, as the mind delivers wounds
(A beautiful god at work by the light of the moon)
Upon the bodies of the men, women, mules and battle hounds.
And all cry out, or bark, or bray, "Let us begin!"
Among the dying circulate two men in black;
And ever do the fires of the dead burn thick
Lighting the room, like a world that is seen
From without, at night, by a philosophic wanderer,
Wherein the beautiful one prepares her bed.

5. By such a light as this.

By such a light as this, in such a room,
We all of us shall read the book of pain
Backward, toward the beginning, a thousand years,
Sleeping or waking—all of us—the same.
Thirty years ago—or more—when I was young
I read, all day, the book as it was written,
And then, by night, page after page of the same
Book in dreams—a student of the other hours:
Iam redit et virgo, "Now returns the maid!"
And the song we sing a little higher;
Redeunt Saturnia regna, "Now the Millennium!"
In the sleep of the beautiful one.
Between the first encounter as in a dream,
An unfeathered arrow, arrow of metal unknown
(The glance of Asenath, lady of pain,
The queen, seeing and being seen—in lace),
And the consummation, there intervene ten thousand
Snowless winters, and death without renown,
(A love, in fact, like any other in a college town)
Wherein a million worlds die and are born,
And all the peoples and the blaze of the face.
Between the assignation and the interview

Expands the time of a long life—my own—
Some dim hilarity—(incongruous,
In any case)—of the conscious soul—
With no clear aim, like an autumnal rain,
The death-in-life of Cambridge pastoral.
It comes to this: the body on a path
Discoursing, drunk or lost in thought (*"Tityre tu"*),
By moonlight to Asenath, the Queen—
A body thrown, as it were, beneath a monument
To be the ultimate inquisitor
Of sentiment before our other hours dawn
And the fires of Millennium are sown.

6. Where is the sun today?

Where is the sun today? Where has he gone?
Far to the South—the sad Miami of the soul—
He is in Opa-Locka at the old King Cole Motel
(These days a coronary hospital)
Feeding the manatees in the canal.
He watches at his ease the fires to the North,
Limps to and fro, concerns himself with "truth,"
Tries verses, as he says, a little doggerel
Devised in tribute to the great MacGonagall:
"Now Old King Cole was a merry old soul
And a merry old soul was he (tweedle dee)
He called for his pipe and he called for his bowl
And the truth in poetry (twee tweedle dee
Tweedle dee). But his motel beside the sea
Is the gate of hell. Love moved its maker
But couldn't pay the bill. I am not dead,
Says the MacGonagall." With this and other
Poetic Gems he entertains the Pelikans.
To him the manatees reply—without remorse:
"There are a million suns like you in the universe
Each with an absolute device, ambiguous
Instructions, and also a suspicious limp,

Signifying impotence—and the 'consolations' of hemp.
Look! Look to the sea! A lady there
(A million suns, or more, shine down on her
And every one is a 'MacGonagall,'
That is to say, a poet without a soul)
Is walking on the sand among her animals.
The children entertain her with their laughter
(The beautiful one, *en grande toilette,* our mother)
Which is why she prefers to live near water."
—Northward the factories are flaming in the dark.
But here in Opa-Locka beside the pool
Two men, fastidious in black despite the weather,
One with a sponge, the other with a knife,
Open and close the gates of hell all summer
And the sun who feeds us, a clumsy fool
With an absolute device—the natural man
Wanted (in any case) by the police—
Watches the Millennium come on and the new life.

7. Above the pages.

Above the pages. . . . Above the table in the room
Where these pages lie . . . a lady hovers and peers
Down, as if to say what new thing is this
Since I died—what new thing has he done
In the last hour before dawn, when the wind
Falls and then hauls round on shore. The day dawns.
And the wind rises, again, bringing odors
Of the salt sea and the sea weed. A lady hovers
And peers, "What new thing?"—The children are gone
From her bosom and the animals from the shadow
Of her knees. Alone in her death and cold,
She gathers her laces against the sea wind,
Turns, and looks down at the writing of her child
(She knows what she likes, dead or alive).
It is as if the universe turned back,
(The greatest poet, in fact the only one),

Stopped on the long walk of her enduring habit
From life to death in the morning twilight
Across a shadowed room toward the high windows
Which open on the gardens and the sea,
And read the pastoral of our misery to the end,
The actual work at night of the left hand.
But I sleep on into the light of day
(A philosophic wanderer among the things of stone
Interrogating the lunar pastorals of Millennium,
"What do I love? What does Love intend?")
With the cold barrel of a loaded gun
(First light, out of the fatal oceans of the night, under wind,
Empty of everything but origin and end,
Or light fallen at noon that detonates upon the ice,
The absolute device of the Autumnal sun)
In my right hand pointed toward my head
Where is, where dwells the lady Asenath—
The mind! Kill her, the Lady of Pain in me.
Kill me, the body at the end of a cold path.
And if anyone ask you, then, any god
Or any philosopher, or any shadow
"What has he done in the night?", "Where has he gone?",
"What does he know?" Say only I have gone to America,
America by moonlight, the beautiful one,
America by the light of the sun.

8. All things visible and invisible.

All things visible or invisible, visible and invisible,
All things before and all things after this time,
Angels and women and men, angels or women and men,
And the visage of their being that shows itself
In war, and the other that shows itself in the Millennium,
Come to the light. We walk, together, through America
(She is wearing—as demanded by the fashion—
Un chapeau cloche in honour of Wallis Simpson,

And carries in her arms a baby with a tiny face
Bundled against the cold and weary of circumcision)
In the new life. "Behold" (I say) "the ruined factories
Of the dawn, the fires now thin, pale and dying
In a rising light (the dying of dying)—and the pyres,
The corpse fires of Apollo's making, and the grave
Person of Egypt, vain of hair and eyes.
The monument presents the angel Metatron,
The angel of the face, the beautiful one,
A tall woman, or a man with turbaned head—"
"I was in heaven," said Asenath, "when Enoch died,
And saw and heard. The *ofanim*, the *seraphim*, the *cherubim*,
All those who move the throne of God and the ministering
Spirits whose substance is consuming fire,
At a remove of six hundred and fifty million
And three hundred parasangs, noticed the presence
Of a human being and exclaimed, 'Whence the odor of one
Born of woman—a grain of incense that perfumes
The universe visible and invisible, and disquiets all things:
The one object of desire (the rest is loss,
Or cosmos) equal to the mind's desire
Of an object, light of the fire by which
The philosophic wanderer at night
(The body on the path that has no motion)
First catches sight of America
Under the moon, and reads the name of the nation?'"
The monument is inscribed on the South side,
"Neither shall there be any more pain,"
And on the West, "First proved to the world Oct., 1846."
"This also cometh of the Lord of Hosts"
Is written on the North, and on the East
The rest is darkened by unseasonable rain. . . .
Walking with mother in the new life
I have explained these and other matters.
Whether she has understood, or not, it is now done.
("There is no angel of the face without a kiss,
No face at all," she says, "unless you make it up, *du fard*.")

Let MacGonagall, the sun, clean up the park.
Let the sea cows make their moan and drown.
Pay me, philosophers, throw me a bone.
Shadows, tell me what passes current in the dark.

9. A fulgurous flash!

A fulgurous flash! *Le remède dans le mal.*
The angry similitude of a thought
(Killing and quickening, leaving him well taught)
Made him awake, as if the light had kissed
His head and left the room, saying nothing,
Never to return. The whole night he had been alone,
God knows where. But at least he had made up
His mind; and the swallow sang to him of Fate
Like Mrs. Simpson in the bath with Edward VIII:
"Here come," she whispers, "the Regulators of the World.
Here come War, Poetry, Law, Religion—
And with some luck (and skill) the duke's erection."
There is an odor in the air of things brought from afar,
Sandalwood, cinnamon, jute, urine, tar,
And Metatron, the angel of the face,
The human form of everything—the Mind
That wrestled with Jacob at the ford of Jabbok
And instructed him in triumph after our kind.
("This night," she said, "no enchantment prevails.")
Metatron is Master of the Work, a youth
With hair (as the Americans say) slicked off the face.
No veils, philosophers, nothing to conclude—
A boy who walked with god and then was not. . . .
Everything has an angel in charge of it;
And when they sing in chorus there rises in the Ether Dome
The iron bells of the ancient tower of Kublai Khan,
O wondrous universe! Then the Millennium
And the purification of women after eight days
And the drowning in the river called Dinur
Of angels who did not sing punctually at the right hour.

And there will be no more sea and no more
Seafaring. And the Mind whom I so deeply love,
The poem of every man and woman who has ever lived,
Will be seen (O beautiful one!) like a moon
In eclipse over America—lady of pain—
Hanging in the empty firmament, a bare flat place;
And the moon will turn once more in the vacant
Universe of love, and wipe the tears
Forever from his eyes and smooth his face. . . .
"Kiss me," she says, "or I'll tear your heart out."
And pastor earth will sing to him and all the countries
Of the world build up his monument because
He answers, with confidence, like a man
In a well-made suit, "My lords and lordly shadows,
And you, fastidious masters of the knife, killing and quickening,
And you, drugged singers of the doggerel of life,
Inscribe it on the East side of the stone:
This happened to me!" And then—*for her*—"TAKE THIS KISS."
And in a flash the hieroglyph is written and erased
(Thus waking thought appears and disappears at dawn
On the great streams of the universe
By an absolute device defaced, or lost
Like dew at the same hour brightening the air
Which the sun draws upward and devours)—: *"ONLY THIS IS."*
—And now the song and the echoes of the song are done.

10. "You must know everything."

Once more we are alone, among the bathers,
On the shore of the sky. And time is hunting us,
Insectivorous time, and there is only infinite space.
No sun, no moon, no dome, no doom, no door,
Only the obscure pathways of a thought
Lead us again and yet again to this shore
Where are traces of fire. Listen! The shepherds
Are whispering in the dark, the weary shepherds
Of the pastoral strayed far from the meadow

Of their common song, by night, into this shadow.
But I say to you, I have done this entertainment
For a reason: in time there will come a time
Whether then you will be sitting on the ground
Or standing against a wall, alone then
Or in company, that the man or woman
Always to your left, but mostly unseen,
Will suddenly come clear and say to you,
"Now it is your turn to sing, here is the instrument."
And then, my dear, you must know everything.

A PASTORAL

At that time the sheep called to him
From their wormy bellies, as they
Lay bloating in the field. He was
A pastoralist,
The schoolhouse hardly handsize
In a sky of flax.

         He began
Then to keep the sayings of man
(The left hand writing; the right hand
Crossing out) farming the time by day
With a great rake
And in the evening hearing myths
Of the hurricane and the tornado
(Straws driven through glass),
And of the waking in the grave
(The sharp hands of brothers buried
Together).

            In the deep night the rat-
Traps in the seed room broke the rat's
Back, and the rat called to him in
The next room over in a penetrating
Eloquent way.

           In the parlor it was
Always deep night where the separated
Organs of the living slept in jars
(The lank goiter and the rotted
Appendix) awaiting the end-time
When the emasculated ram will rise
In the flax-blue sky
(Cold as the final bluing of a Sunday wash)
And all of us will know
The use in beauty of the whole body.

In the hay field was the beginning
Of knowledge:
Sour wine, the great rake hoisted
Toward the high sun-altar of the stack
And the hoist rope hauled out hard
(Like a greased whip of which the stories
Told were of the severing of limbs)
By two staggering teams—and the whole
Sun in its extreme tower of noon.

All he heard was violent and sad
But he kept on writing the sayings
Of man with his left hand, and sent
Them off in broken words, and waited
In the mortal field
Listening to the mice in the bottom
Of the stack.

        Now though the schoolhouse
Hangs like a stone over the field
Robed in its winding sheet as blue as air,
The shepherd hand of eloquence still keeps
And flashes
Out the sayings of the man—
And the other (the right hand of
Obliterating habit) sleeps.

FLAX

A Ballad of Schools and Dreams

If the desire of men and women is to know—if *that*
Is our passion—the action of the sun and moon, the action
Of earth and ocean, and histories of the theory of rain:
Then let the poem of the knowledge we desire be hooded
And buried among the secrets of the snow, in the treasuries
Of the rain, and be neither living nor dead. —But the fields
Are covered with snow, and then again white with the risen grain;
The linnet is mad for the mystic seed of the blue flax flower;
And all over the nation the singers are sitting, or standing,
Or walking up and down, or in their beds, alone or in company,
Awake or in their dreams. The nation of the singers is
A great nation, living and dead! What difference in the nation
Of the singers distinguishes the living and the dead?
How shall we know them? They are so much alike. All suffer,
Pay debts, exact revenge, whisper among themselves, and utter
Poems. If you ask them, the living singer may say, "I am dead";
And the dead most certainly will say, "I am alive. Alive!"
One mark alone distinguishes the dead among the singers:
The dead among the singers do not know *The Song of the Lord*.
They have built for themselves solitudes. If you go among them,
As you should, putting your questions, asking for songs, the tall
Singer will sing the tall song of the high streams above;
And the oak singer, so slow to grow, indicates the lightning;
And the bitter singer sings praises of the death singer
At certain hours.

　　　　—But I have seen at a distance—looking to
The right, as one walks eastward, where the road rises between
Two fields making a hill—the school house, daughter of the hill,
In a field of flax, in a sixth year when the flax is blue;
And I have heard at the same distance the children singing
In the school room: "In heaven's name," they sing, "can you, perhaps,
Impart to me some power to enable me to bear this force

Emerging from my heart." Or they cry out, "Help me! Help me!"
Or they whisper: "I wish you were dead." "I wish you were alive."
(In the daytime, I pronounce these words silently. In the night
I say them aloud.) And on the school room floor something is
Coming to pass at long last. The teacher, neither a man
Nor a woman, turns to the window and looks left down the hill,
Seeing the boy at the road's edge, who has seen and heard, rise
From where he was sitting with his question ("Mother, O Mother!
If I run faster is the way shorter?" The mother thinks a little,
And then she says, "No, dear."), and begins to walk to his right.
As he walks, the maize erects itself. The corn and other grasses
Inherit the whitening grain, and the signs of heaven are abundant:
"Let the school house be built in a quiet place, perhaps a field."
As he walks, the sun weaves and unweaves the blue garment we know,
And the two moons, the bright and the obscure, inscribe and devour
Our stony scripture, the Servant's Tale read by its own light:
"Work then while it is day," it says, "for the night cometh when
No man can work."

       —As he walks, between the maize and the corn,
The rain comes and goes, and the hurricane. As he walks on,
He hears the voice of the teacher, "Hurry. You will be late!"
Before him rises the hill, bitter and high. O the hill!
The hill so hard to climb! In the morning he sees the stones
Of the road. At noon he sits among the flowers at the roadside,
Among their tombs, on which are written in a flowery hand
"Remember me!" And he sees below in the valley as the day fades,
A general and his soldiers, some absolutely calm, and others
Garlanding flowers for the feast that they will hold in Hades.
The night cannot be told. But at the dawn he sees by the moon
Of the imagination, thin and cold, the serpent in the dust
Awaiting the heat of the sun. The boy turns on the road,
Enters the school and takes his place. The daughter of the hill
Gives him a kiss. The children are singing now of the Lord
In his solitude. (Something is coming to pass, as it must,
In the blue light.) The linnets contribute the upper voice
Of the song. And the low chorus of the grasses, the wind
That is always going on, and the solemn action of the sun

And moon supply the bourdon. Today it's raining where I am.
The hill's fair daughter—the maiden in the tower—still summons.
And I am like the singer, among the singers I have heard:
That great woman I once heard cry, "O Mother, I have sung
Every word of the song that you taught me by fire and sword.
The day is at an end, and I am out of breath. May I go out
To play now by myself." The mother thinks a little. Then
She says, "No, my dear. Now you must sing *The Song of the Lord.*"

A SUMMER DAY

After a long time and much wandering
The mind returns to its first world and last,
Naked as a worm, dressed up like the president;
And there our mother is, at her window still!
"Welcome," she says. "It is a Summer day."
—Inside the mother is a moated garden,
And in the mother garden there are other
Gardens—shade-gardens and sun-gardens. And
Above the garden gate is plainly written,
"Summoned or unsummoned a god is here."
Our mother is old, and the gardens are dying.
The moat is drunk by the hydroptic lily.
The last pregnancy of the world has come
To term—and ultimate light is everywhere.
Inside the gardens stray the mother's mothers,
Women of the gardens, who turn and sigh
In Summer light. "Where are the lordly men
And women who throve on earth before our time,
And their thoughts that were hopeful and unhopeful?
For they were aware of the things of the world—
Mosquitoes in the shade-gardens, of course,
And something they could not name out there
In the dark among the pipsissiwas;
And they had their works and days (did they not?)
And are underground, or are perhaps the stars."
—The questions narrow, even as they sharpen
And point. "Where are those who live among us *now*
As lovers, or friends, and seem the outcast shadows
Of our questionable souls, moving or still,
Or unmoving, or unstill? Where are they?"
I think they are translated backward toward
The silent birthstool of great age, and thrown
Like runic damage on a rain-worn stone
That all may read, in times to come, the history
Of our Summer day, in the language of the born.

"But where *are* those who will come after us?"
The women turn and sigh, "Where are you, children?
What steers by night the ship of the return,
Among islands, and through the gates of dream—
The iron, the ivory, and the horn?"
—This is the millennium of the gardens.
The mother is dying who remembered us
And the gardens, sun and shade, and the sighing
Women, and the god leaning to the dark.
In my beginning, I arose from a bed
In which I did not lie down; in my end
I lie down in a bed from which I shall
Not arise, dressed up like the president,
Sleepless with expectation all night long.

MARY SNORAK THE COOK, SKERMO THE GARDENER, AND JACK THE PARTS MAN PROVIDE DINNER FOR A WANDERING STRANGER

There is as much holiness now as there ever was
And there is as much fire now as there ever was
And as many locusts in the desert and bees
But there is no hope for the oaks. The winds fall
From a greater height, a heavier burden on their streams.
And the day darkens. When it grows too dark to read,
The sun having set, we begin to write—for *that*
We do not need our eyes—and continue still
The history of the stranger, Mind, that spends
His force on the immortal seas in search of a companion
Who is like himself, and finds nothing like himself,
Island after island. Welcome him! Welcome him!
He is the only stone that can be solitary
In the universe: a man of stone on a sea of shadows,
Worthy of a history inscribed in the dark.
By day he reads the Book of the Wandering Stranger
To regulate desire, until the dark comes on,
Turning the dead leaves like a restless wind.
All through the afternoon, at ease among faint recognitions,
He pronounces the syllables. "The beauty of it,
The beauty of it all." By night he swims
On immortal seas and visits the world
(Temples, towns, seaports, ponds, and wells)
A man of stone, subject of histories,
And yet how changed, how fallen from what he was.
The Mind is fallen, and travels in a blind disguise
(Above him the maelstrom of the holy ocean
And beneath a storm of fire in the skies),
Companionless wanderer in the dark. —Welcome him!
An undistinguished fragment of the greater thought,
A common flower on a barren hill, or stone by chance
Discovered at the shore—for no clear reason
Carried home—and somehow lost—forgotten on the sill

Of a summer bedroom or given away to an indifferent guest—
And now witness to the Millennium:
A stone of witness to the one world that is.
—Who will make the dinner, then, for the man of stone
And who arrange his pastoral? How is it done?
The gardener supplies the food, the "wreckage" of his hoe,
A person almost mute, not a reader, name of Skermo.
The cook is cheerful, dressed in a printed sack
(*Pillsbury Flour,* 500 lbs.). Her name is Mary, Mary Snorak,
So fat she sneaks out *sidewise* through the doorway
When she wants a smoke. Mary is in love with Jack,
The parts man, who likes his dinner (in fact, the only guest),
Good for a joke. For after all the Mind must dine alone
And find nothing like, until dawn breaks with a crack
Against the seashore where he lies among the stones,
Dreaming of the immortal ocean, and reading in the afternoons
The Book of the Wandering Stranger written in the dark.
Holy, holy, holy is the lordly host
And holy is witness Mind, "historic traveller," and guest.
But holiest of all the fools who arrange the feast,
Skermo the gardener, the parts man Jack, and sidewise Mary
Snorak who loves him as he is, and can take a joke.

SPRING SONG OF THE BEHEMOTH

One of us—who have not had time to think
Since the beginning of the world—beholds
The ocean. From vertiginous chalk cliffs,
Like a suicide of two minds, his gaze
Lurches and falls to the glassy sea a long
Way down. He is happy, now, not to have
Knowledge of the pain of other souls, or
The greater pain of other bodies, not even
His own in which he only partially
Recognizes the man, at best a companion—
Older, darker, perhaps feminine,
(Perhaps divine!). A gentle breeze springs up
Behind him from the land, smelling of gorse
And the hairbells of the down, and on its stream
Small flakes of a spectacular late snow.
His coat is heavy with the soil of the sea
And torn by its long nail; yet he is happy
To escape the strait waters of the passage.
For every creature of the land there is
Another of its kind in ocean, out there
In the glare of the sun, beginning far below
His feet and stretching away without end,
Breathing and thinking as it folds at every breath
A private history on every shore.
Untimely born, the snow of April rises
And falls in the face of the Spring which stares
Like a blinded girl in the presence of the
Visible god, lifting up her brows without a reason
To the wasted virtuosity of heaven . . .
—The man has come to the edge of the world
And stopped, as it were, to think on the cliffs;
And out of the breakers rises the shout
Of Behemoth "Ha Ha Ha Ha," as if another
Man, and yet the same, a lustrous shadow,
Was tirelessly tossing his white arms still,

His long coat heavy with the soil of water
And a nail in his heart. Consider the jeweled
Plates of the body, as it was in the beginning
Of the world, and tune your fork to the *cantus*
Of the thought "Ha Ha Ha"! As for the man
On the chalk cliffs with suicidal gaze:
He hangs his dripping garments up—a trophy
To the Master of the world and all hard ways.

POLAND OF DEATH (I)

I hear my father underground scratching with a nail. And I say,
"Father, here is a word." He says, "It does not help. I am
Scratching my way with a nail ever since you dug me down
In the grave, and I have not yet come to Poland of death."
And I hear my mother saying, "Sing me something about the
Forest primeval." So I say, "Mother, here is a story."
And she says, "I have a pain in the blind eye, the left one
Which is dead."

       I hear my father scratching with a nail again,
And I offer him the words of a song, first one word and then
Another, and he refuses them. He says, "It is not a word," or
"It is just a word," or "It is not what you feel." "What
Do you feel?" Poland of death! Ever since I put my father
In the grave he has been scratching a way, and has not yet
Got under the sea, and mother has a pain in her blind eye.

So I tell her the story of a woman named Irene: How when she
Walked into a hayfield behind her house the animals shrieked.
How when she crossed over to the other side of the field
The clothes in the bluing froze, and all the yeast died
In the potato water. How when she reached the edge of the forest
Everything went up in flames in the farm she had left behind.
Then my father underground says, "Do not be bewildered by
The surfaces. In the depths, everything is law." And I say,
"My true love in the grave-deep forest nation is a forester."
And mother says, "This is the forest primeval." Poland of death!

POLAND OF DEATH (II)

As not in life my father appeared to me
Naked in death and said, "This is my body."
So I undressed and faced him, and we were
Images of one another for he

Appeared to me at the same age I am.

Then he said, "Now I am in Death's country."
And I saw behind him in the dogmatic
Mirror of our death a forest of graves
In morning light. The smoky air was full
Of men and women sweeping the stone sills.
"Since you dug me down in America,"
He said, "I've been scratching a way with a nail,
And now I have come to Poland of death."

And I saw the keepers of the graves moving
Among the shadows and the lights like lights.

Then he said to me—and not for the first time—
"Give me a word." And again, "Who are you?"
And then, after a long silence, "Write me
The Black Book of the world." And I replied,
"Louis, here is my body." And then one
Of us grew erect, and the cries began—
Like the weak voices of disembodied children
Driving crows from the cornfields.

                          —He showed me
The severed head of a mother in her tears
Kissing and eating the severed head of a child;
And one familiar spirit like a snarled hank
Of somebody's black hair. And he showed also
A bloody angle of the wires where groans
Of men and women drowned the roar of motors

And mounted to a prophecy. Then he gave me
A sharp look and said, "Thank God, I have no children,"
And ran off with a cry down an alley of
That place like one who remembered suddenly
The day of his own death—

A short, pugnacious man, but honest and reliable.

Night fell and the mirror was empty for a while.
Then appeared, or half-appeared, Beatrice, my mother,
In the bed of her great age.
When she sleeps her human eye closes, and rests:
But her blind eye—the dead one—stares out
As if to say, "This is the forest primeval.
This is Death at last."

And I saw again the keepers of the graves
Moving among the shadows and the lights.

POLAND OF DEATH (III)

The dead are beyond caring. But Beatrice
Is not beyond caring. She is not dead.
She says to Death, "You are *nothing* to me."
She writes it down, "I won't stay." "I'm not old."
"This necropolis is a *disgrace.*" "I don't know
These people. And (besides) the country is cold."
Poland of death! Our mother is a homeless soul
Who multiplies worlds. What does Beatrice see?
With her right eye she superintends the facts:
Forests and lakes. —Beatrice has a book
In which she notes each Spring the day and hour
The lake-ice disappears. *It does not annihilate.*
Blackened by the rains of the equinox,
It rots and bruises like the abused skin
Of a tormented animal, and then descends
And rests, as the metal does in a mirror
With the sky in it and a little wind,
On the bottom where the meanings are
Compassionless, allegorical, absorbed
And like her mind incapable of death.
Such was her superintendence of the years.
But now she has descended with the ice
Beneath the shadows of the pleasure boats
And dwells in the metal with the ancestors.
Her tears mingle with the freshness of the streams,
Wept for primeval forests in the darkness where
All the prisoners rest together, out of the air,
Wept from the left eye of our mother (the dead one),
In its dream of other worlds in the Millennium.
—After a while she says to Death, *"Now come!"*
(She has crossed her knees, fixed her hair with a comb,
And drawn an afghan over her face like fate.)
But he will not come. Her "offense" is great.
Death says repeatedly, *"You do not love me, Bea!"*
He also says to her, "I am your only son."

"My brother!" I reply (astonished), "I understand you.
But you must do this *for our sake*. Mother Beatrice,
A woman of strong will, multiplies worlds."
Then Death spoke for the last time, and was precise.
"*I* believe," Death says, "in the one world that is."
"And *I* read" (he adds) "in the literal of ice."
At once the forests of Poland began to blow,
Scattering leaves far out across the lake,
Dead leaves with the faces of men and women
In their multitudes, each one subject of prophecy.
Thus, two principles of art contend. The land-
Scape bends. Everything that is takes sides.
And I myself cry out, taking my brother's part,
"Keep it simple, please—so we can understand!"
And hear our mother calling in strange tones
Across black water, against the storm: "Adorn!
Adorn the necropolis, and sweep the sill,"
Calling to her stubborn son who hates her, her only one,
And will not kill her, or take her home, or mourn.
—And so I say to all of you, whoever you are,
Sons and daughters on the hills and at the shore
Who see the storm sublime in Spring year after year
And note the tossing of the deathless limb of care
("This is the worst place I've ever lived in."
"I want", she says, "a clean house and a quiet town."),
Honor the poet who turns the ancient quern
Of tears, the salt mill of the mother's cry.
My brother and I—the sons of Beatrice—
We multiply the worlds—who is now ice.

POLAND OF DEATH (IV)

1.

It is the duty of every man,
And woman, to write the life of the mother.
But the life of the father is written by
The father alone. —Now he is of great size
In Poland of Death, and his garment is sewn
Of superior cloth. I came upon him down
An alley of that place, sitting on a wall,
At the intersection of two walls, looking wise:
Known there as Louis of Minneapolis,
The *maître à pensée* of the necropolis.
And his song was, "When the deep purple falls. . . ."

2.

As I came up, he cast me a sharp glance
And stopped short at the middle of the verse
("Sleepy garden walls . . .")—meaning, "This is
Your last chance to say something." "*Say* something!"
"How do you like my suit?" And so I say
To him, "You looked better naked and small."
And he says, "What's given here can never be
Refused, or lost. That's the rule. Take this nail!"
Then he started an old song I didn't like
At all. Something of the "matter of the race"—
At very least the long and sonorous breath

3.

Of a dark language. —O Poland of Death!
I asked a beggar-woman of the cemetery
What he sang, the young one smelling of sea

And milk who sweeps the sill. "Louis," she replies,
"Is a proud Jew now, dwelling among the dead,
A big Rabbi of rats dressed in a suit
That fits. A prince!" And then—before my eyes—
On the vapors of the universe—the head
Of Louis hung—like Brutus, the conspirator;
And its song poured back centuries of rain
From the Etruscan jar of an old man's voice

4.

Into the water-wells of the abyss:
"Now I know everything," it sang, "being in
The right place! —How did I get so wise?
When I proceeded Doctor of Philosophy
Torches smoked and flamed from every tower.
(Let the flame leap up, the heart ignite and burn!)
The celebrations of commencement were elaborate,
And I was clothed then, as you see me now,
In a suit that fits, sewn of superior cloth,
Invulnerable to the rust, the moth,
And the diurnal changes of the light

5.

In the air. My boy, the truth is great."
"Louis," I cried, "soon I am going to die.
The world is nearing its end. Say something
I can understand!" So he pulled out a beret
Of reddish brown, put it on his head, and smiled
Like a prince, as the woman said, or king—
(Of grave-diggers, as it seems, or wolves or Jews).
And I heard, then, the father calling to the son
And the son responding to the father from afar,
And the daughter to the mother, and the mother
To the children—voices like falling water,

6.

Or the shadow of swans, the sigh of the swan's feather:
"After a thousand years the Devil will be loosed
On a day, and in the morning of that day
This Louis will ride forth in his 1950
Chevrolet of prophecy—with feet, hands,
And four on the floor (Ezekiel I).
And the Rektor of the University
The Archbishop, the Lord Mayor and the General
Of Artillery, will applaud his face
And he will meet the host in the air,
Igniting the *auto-da-fé* of the sun."

7.

But all I understood, in fact, was the next phrase
On of the song he was singing as he sat
At the intersection (you will remember it)
Of two walls, "When the deep purple falls."
This time he got as far as the "nightingales."
Then stopped, and shouted, "This is the story
Of my life. I am the Professor now
Bigger than the Lord God. *He* was seduced
And made the world against His will—by art.
My son, I never married. I have no children.
I was smart. My father was a butcher, an empiricist

8.

Who knew the Law. (And that explains, in case
You want to *know*, why I hate cats! . . .)
When the end comes, like a dark wife at last,
It will be among the nightingales and rats
Of the necropolis, as the 'purple' falls
On Poland of Death." He turned his face, then,

And stopped his voice, never to speak again.
The Etruscan jar rang. I said to him: "Louis
I will sing you a new song." And the abyss
Supplied its word, "Halleluya!" *Praise
The Lord.* Then the beggar-woman of the cemetery

9.

Saw her chance, and gave the old man on the wall
A proper kiss. For what? For being wise,
And (after all) unmarried, and for dressing well.
Happy, happy Louis! The new song was this:
"Father, not father, *O roi magicien!*
Mother, not mother, O name of Beatrice!
Does the cloth forget the weaver, does the field
Of millet in its season no longer remember the sower,
Or the birds that feed on it honor in later summer
The labor that laid it down? O Yes! And the pot
The woman's hand who made it has forgot.

10.

How much less the mind, reading and running hard,
Touches the world. (O touch me, *roi thaumaturge!*)
Therefore, Louis of Minneapolis at ease upon a wall,
Sucking on a nail—the Jew in charge—
Demands a word when the deep purple falls.
What do I hear? An audible air of voices
Calling out and answering: *'Au revoir,
Ma femme chère,' 'Mon frère,' 'Ma soeur,' 'Mon père.'*
What do I see? Poland of Death! Louis driven out
(The Doctor in his garment of superior cloth)
Into the field behind the wall and shot!

11.

'What is the past?' 'What passes?' 'What is to come
When I have died?' . . . *What is to come?* No figure
Has it yet, no form. —Night falls in a room.
Someone in the dark is scratching with a nail:
The chronicler. Upon the road to the necropolis
Approaches always the chrome of battlecars,
Convertibles in columns like descended stars.
What is the past? —Night falls in a room. A king
Gives laws in the abyss on a drowned throne.
What passes? —The *auto-da-fé* of the sun.
What is the WORD? Halleluya. The Lord is ONE."

POLAND OF DEATH (V)

1.

There are many waves when there is wind at sea.
Each wave has a history which ends, it seems, at the shore.
Or it begins again, there, in another form—in thunder,
Or in a proverb, or with a sigh. On the shore are
Often many stones. What then? *What then?* Each one is
Perfect, and each is a cause of dissatisfaction to me.
Each one is whole and each is a fragment of a greater whole,
Finite or infinite stones: minds, or glimpses of mind.
Which one is the stone of witness? For one is the stone
Of witness. It may or may not be on this shore, or on
The countless shores everywhere. But where it is it hears
The proverb of the waters on windy nights in Summer,
And at noon in Autumn watery sighs, and on Winter mornings
The thunder of the wave when there is wind at sea.
In Spring the stone of witness sees the wave fall down
Upon the shore. And then rise from its fall, shaken,
In another form, and climb to the shore road which it
Crosses—to hear the blackbirds sing in the marshland.

2.

—How hard, then, to know the greater poet! And the work
Of the greater poet? How shall I know what it is?
And if I know what it is, how shall I make it known,
Scratching with this nail? How shall I make it known
To you? And if I make it known to you, what then shall
I do? How shall I endure my pain and your pain,
Knowing the greater poet and the work? Is it like
A tree that casts no shadow and bears no fruit,
And yet is all shadow and all the fruit there is?
Is it, perhaps, the fatal earth: a stone colossus
Made by mind that stands for all the dead, and stands?

Its name? "The One"? "The Dark"? —To make a beginning
I drew up an advertisement which I posted throughout
Baku, that great city, with the help of small children
(Also in x, y, and z, up and down the Transcaspian Line):
"The Universal American Travelling Workshop
Will stop here, in its passage, for a very short
Time. Makes, alters, and repairs everything. . . ."

3.

Why? Why do this? Why this device? —In another life,
I was a very sad young woman named Irene. I saw her *once!*
She was standing alone ("Such is the mind," I thought,
"When it is known."), like a young tree of an exotic kind
In a late season. Bride of the shadow, daughter of the sun.
Dressed up for evening in the bazaar at noon. At her feet
For Sale was a box with a dark lid which I bought.
No questions asked. In it was an Edison phonograph together
With numerous rolls. Among those still intact,
Some were recorded and others blank. What did
She mean? What did she lack? Why was she selling this
Machine which multiplies worlds? "For sure" (I said)
"Among them is my mother's life: The ballad songs
Of her girlhood in Kansas, or on the Mountains of the Moon;
The odes and elegies of her middle age, as wife *titrée*
Of Louis of Minneapolis, *maître à savoir;*
And then her lyric, last, demented wanderings unseen
By air? Peace be to thy burning house, Irene,

4.

From thee and thy machine incessant waters of repair
Pour down in streams out of your floral horn
Among the Asiatic customers of Sears. For much was broken
In Baku, Kizil-Arvat, and Ashkhabad and Andijan
Up and down the roadbed of the Transcaspian line.

Lord! What on earth they did not bring. An apparatus
For plucking out grey hairs and one for stoning cherries;
Another one for grinding copper sulphate to sprinkle on
The sweat zones of the body; also a device for striking
Matches; one for melting ice; and a "galvano-plastic" cabinet
For forming artificial flowers, and masks of the dead
From plaster, feathers, wax or bread. —Don't you see?
Thinking is hard, harder than we imagined in our youth.
There is no god of writing. Or he is overtaken by
The police and jailed (or worse) in the name of "truth."
Forlorn Irene dressed up for evening with fire in her hair
From whom I bought the box with the dark lid in another life,
Irene, guide to the mother's mind! Irene, power of repair!

5.

Nobody's wife! They are dancing in Baku at noon in the bazaar
To the roll that repeats the circulation of the air,
Souvenir of the Chicago Fair (1893) and called "The Mind
As It Is Known" or "The Stone": witness to the mother's life
That mends the soul. And the machines are singing to the note
And song, like blackbirds in the marshland all day long.
The work is going on. All honor then to The Universal American
Travelling Workshop of the Transcaspian! —Oh! It is hard. But
You see now, do you not? How it does not pertain—our "alive."
How our "alive" does not pertain—to this world or that one—
Neither to the above or underground—to America or Palestine
Or the Code Napoléon. To Avalon, or ocean. Or to the truth.
The mystery is in the continuation. The train is going North.
Poland of Death! The engine is drawing it to fatal earth.
The stone is in the mouth of the great god, poet divine
And what the song will be nobody knows. Thunder in the air.
Sighs along the ground. A proverb (something about a fool)
In the right hand of the son. And in his left, a nail.

MRS. O'LEARY'S CAT

When they built the city Ur of utter light
Where before that the shore was like a face
Without feature the Tree of Intention was
Raising itself above out of the wells
And the graves were empty of the first death.
That night everybody in the household,
All the sleepers, dreamed of a great wave.
Toward morning one of us dreamed of a birth.
Then, the old cat of the house awoke and went out
Into the snow, signifying his displeasure,
Having "business in the city." The sun rose
Like a lutanist who has played all night
And is pale and weary—done with the music.
We gathered at the birth-bed where the dreamer lay:
"I dreamed the dream," she said, "of having borne
Your child. A daughter. *Now, she must have a name
Or she will die.*" —Thereafter, it was sun
By day and moon by night. Night after night
The weary lutanist built up the city Ur
By means of hooks and grapples in his song,
And the Tree of Intention flowered among the stars.
But the mother labored at the name in vain
And the child grew thin. "Perhaps," we said,
"Her father is the King of Prussia and her name
Is Fredrick or she is the fallen aviatrix,
Amelia Earhart, resurrected from the wave.
Or Lilith, the first made woman. Or Lenore,
Or Sappho, or Angelique. Or maybe Snow."
Then, the old cat floated the name "Chicago,"
And the child was saved! The citizens of Ur
Fell silent. They all fell silent and looked about.
The milk in the mother's breasts began to flow
Like a long, indefinite ray of light
On a day that has no color to its light
(Not utter light but light eloquent and slow,

The life of light, passing as it were toward shadow).
And the infant slept that night in the arms of fame
Despite the thunderous labors of the sun
Wrecking the granite ashlar of the shore.
Then, the old cat of the house, having said
His say, went out again with fire in his eye,
Having "business in the city" as before
During the day. The great Tree uttered a cry.
And the burning of the city Ur began.
—O Ur of utter light! Ur of the Chaldee!
A flaming countenance is your fiery shore.
Child of the wave and naiad of the wells,
Because you are as changeable as water
You will be murdered by a passionate man
(Chicago of the mother's mind, my daughter)
And enter the grave of the first death—young!
Where the old cat sleeps on the polished sill
At noon, and the weary lutanist repairs his song,
Until night falls on Ur and on the Tree
Summoning his slaves to the Orphic mill.

OUT OF THE BLUE

(a river doggerel)

Nur in dem Fluss der Gedanken und des Lebens haben die Wörter Bedeutung

I.

Out of the blue! A lyre of seven languages!
Or more! What? Is it the soul? I see it.
Like steel or ocean (our universal destination)
It flows in its own direction, in several
Motions at our feet, as thinking is urgent
And sometimes quick but for the most part slow.

Out of the well below, the blue throne of
The marshland, grave waters rise, swell, and then
Go down—to turn a prophetic mill by falling
In its arms: "It is not your duty to complete
The work. Neither are you free to desist
From it." It says, "O soul! The time is short.

The work is great. The laborers weary. The master
Of the house is urgent"—like thought. Look up!
The day lights of the mill dim, flicker and go out.
The looms fake, falter, and stop. The threads
Tangle and break, because the flow of the stream
Is blocked by a corpse on the grate. —In the dark

II.

The waters speak—ancient habits of the mind,
In several languages, address the work.
The center of the stream proceeds from left
To right, eloquent (stately, bright, and blind):

Capable of our life—by day the common song;
By night the mother tongue, capacious ship

Of light ("Never die" "Never die"). Look down!
Along the shores the direction of the main
Flow reverses. And water goes up stream
In tiny galaxies, like mystic clocks
Tangled in roots and slime that stop and start
And stop before our eyes, telling enormous

Narratives of time: *"Gigantic boatmen come
And go."* Above the clocks small mists erect
Themselves like lunar storms. And over all
The rain falls down, sown by a gentle wind,
Speaking in tongues the bright matter of water:
"We know of life under the gentle wind,

III.

The sower's hand. We know of life in the storm,
The hurricane. But there is a storm beyond
The storms we know, by no measurable degree."
O Lyre of seven languages! What do
The gigantic boatmen cry across the flow?
How do they greet one another? "Yo!", one calls,

"Yo, phantom! What does he fear?" "The hardness
Of the work" is the reply (out of the blue),
"The impending war, the darkening hour,
And the Godforsakenness of the Jew."
This said, the phantoms disappear each paddling
His own canoe, the one with strength upstream

In the direction of the throne, the other falling
Downward to our right where is the mill.
"Yo, phantom!" (the last cry) "What is the word?"
"When He is God" (the last reply) "they are forsaken.

And in the measure He is God—forsaken.
When He ceases to be God they will be comforted

IV.

And wipe the tears forever from their eyes,
Forever lost." Thus pass the gigantic boat-
Men in the dying light, speaking of light
And what the stream carries, what the mill weaves
Then and now, now and hereafter: the sentence
Of the soul. Such is, indeed, the discourse

Of the noble messenger, one having power
With the Lord of the throne, the throne secure.
The sentence of the soul lights up the world!
"Yo, Jew! The light is over all the bright
Matter of water. The light exceeds, surrounds,
Does overflow. Hasten while it is true,

You fool! Because there is a storm beyond
The storm you know." —But now the thin material
Flow of soul is stopped by a corpse on the grate.
It is stopped. No work is done at the mill.
The agent engine that supplies the loom
Of prophecy receives no force, and weaves

V.

No fate. —A woman in her tears under the throne
Has dreamed the dream of extreme storm: when the body
Wakes to find the body *true,* the storm beyond
The storm we know, by no measurable degree. She
Was swept down, in the hour before dawn,
And drowned in the great flood out of the blue,

And darkened the mill, and stopped the loom of prophecy,
Dream of the Jew. Therefore, the stream is dumb
In the nation and goes down to the ocean,
Our destination, silently. The clock strikes
But there is no work. The laborers are weary.
Nothing is done. There is a corpse on the grate

And fear in the heart. —The one gigantic boatman
(*Leichenträger*) has gone down to clear the grate
And start the loom. The other stands beneath
The throne and hears *this note and that one*
(The material flow of thought that drives the work)
At the beginning where the waters speak . . .

VI.

O Lyre of seven languages, or more!
The mastery must be (as I have said elsewhere)
In the continuation. In the dark
The children knot the thread, reset the loom.
And stare at us. It is true true true true,
All the children have blue eyes—every one—

And stare out of the blue. What shall I say!
What can be *done?* The meaning of the world
Is being made in defiance of the Jew.
The boatman lifts the corpse, the wreckage of the storm.
The day lights of the mill flicker and re-illume.
The rivers flow. Nor can I much detain

Them as they pass under the sower's hand,
The windy rain. Night falls. "Yo, Jew, revoke
Thy *tristia.* Here comes the capacious ship
Of light—on time—out of the blue. Look!
The orchestra on deck strikes up a song,
'The Meaning of the World.' The mother tongue!"

Envoy

O lyre of seven languages. Or more!
The continuation is in fact unknown,
"Unknown"—the very word summons the dawn:
A woman in her pain *forever lost*
Still climbs the extreme storm on a sharp stair
High up!—to the blue throne of the marshland,
Where the terms of life begin their *fall*
("Only in our world is the light visible,
Only in the flow of the material soul.")
Down stream, in several motions, to the mill
And after that the ocean—our destination.
What do I know? The body on the grate
That stops the loom, and breaks the thread,
Puts out the light of prophecy, and blocks
The flow of the *mother tongue* . . . is the dead
End of the imagination ("Adore
The throne, and clear the grate. Work, Jew, while it
Is light!"), —and the beginning of all song.

PHOENIX

(Fragment: *Dichterberuf*)

Nascitur arabiis ingens in collibus infans
Et dixit levis aura: "Nepos est ille Jugurtae."

On Arabian hills a monstrous child is conceived,
And the winds say, "It is the grandson of Jugurta."

Rimbaud

—The night awakens images. Day sleeps
On the high bed of music. The century
Is ending and the Millennium. Now
It is all one thought from beginning to end.
What will the hours *mean* in the next world?
For the gods are not attracted to us.
Have they forgotten that we were beautiful
And are still, and that Eternity
Loved us for a reason and Time hates us
Who is in love with Eternity?
There can be no more sleep. Or let the day
Have it, or Death which names nothing at all,
Or the lovers of music. The century is ending
And the Millennium. And Time is enraged.

This is a poem of high places, murderous
Pursuit, atrocious pain, and study of night
And day and the thunder which follows after
With the voices of dogs. Climb to a high
Place. And then throw yourself down. Thus, in the
Terror of the falling death, the illusions
Of day are overcome and dying wakes. Do not
Console yourselves that the gods are dead.
They are enraged, and storm in the tenements
Of the Great Mind night and day. It is all
One thought. The Millennium is calling through

A thousand voices, and to the poet first of all,
Child of Eternity and Time—the unbegotten
Who is present, always, at her own begetting:

First, the shifting of invisible waters
On the bed of waters and the *susurrus*
Of the great wing of light and the lesser wings
That follow it, the Phoenix of Eternity
In flames and insectivorous Time. Then,
The engines of arrival, slamming of doors,
And vast echoing of possible courses
Among which is the sound of many foot falls,
Each one a voice. The last, the signature of *you*.
And so begins again the work of the world
On the high bed of music—murderous pursuit,
The falling of two who enter the storm
Of the Great Mind (horror of Millennium).
And the thinking above all, *thinking* that is

Of the night only—and the new order
Of our other hours in the world unknown.
In one another's arms, we enter the storm
Of the great Mind, the man and woman alone
In sexual union:—a poetic will
In labor toward the consummation of
A single thought, our beauty (O Golden Bird!),
The one thought in the hurricane of thought.
Big winds wind the horologe of the world
Like a stopped clock and the gods are seen
In their tenements—the Phoenix who loves us,
And insectivorous Time in love with Eternity.
So do you not forget, not even if
They have forgotten, to summon the poets.

It is their duty to indicate the hiding
Place of things. Say to them, "Poets! Show us
The lock, the hieroglyph, the seal so we can
See the hiding place of things: the black well

Of their heavens where they sleep. Speak to us
Of the seal and the unglossable poem of the seal.
Write us the enigma of Millennium."—But
I shall not devise an ending. It is un-
Written. Nobody knows the Millennium:
The one pastoral of our other hours signed
With the legible signature of *you*,
O Golden Bird! —Look! the mind of the wind
Is abroad on the great plains of dream. By
Day, small birds hunt the insects of the field

Here and there across the oceanic barley
And among the ripening corn. By night,
As if far off, is heard the voices of dogs.
We lie together on the high bed of music
In utter solitude, our beauty in our arms,
An unbegotten witness, at the end of time,
Under the shadow of the Phoenix wing

A MUSIC LESSON

Once more I hear the voices of the women
Like desert waterfalls long after rain
Still going on among the flowers and the seeds
Of flowers, and hear the voices of the men
Shouting in astonishment far down the valleys
Where the same waters enter into stones and hang
Between the skin and the strangled heart of stone
Until night freezes the dew and the heart
Breaks free, and hear also (or overhear) the voices
Of the dead and the unborn—that mingle where the same
Waters of the rain on inland mountains far away
Flow to the salt sea—pronounce to one another
In my name of time and the world to come.

Companionable voices! I hear you now:

Every tribe has its music. But there is music
That wanders seeking its tribe: —that hangs
Like dust for blazing centuries over a strait place
Among rainless winds, awaiting impatiently
Lost caravans of somnambulant traders
In salt and gold;—that utters irenic law
To the angels of the nations in their killing clothes
(Each nation has an angel with dead eyes)
Deafened by their prophets and singers of songs;
—That writes far out on the disturbed *altum* of ocean
Faint poems of the male spirit floating in air
Through whose penis spindrift music flows
Like semen on the way to human form. Thus
We are sent on errands, known and unknown,
Possible or impossible, as the music finds us.
It is as the soul is, or the mind, in pain
That labors to be acquainted (if it can)
With the barbarous discourse of a mortal brain . . .

O come and see an uninstructed spirit,
New to the instrument, practicing to be
A woman or a man who builds like a lofty song
The one great thing imagined by us impossible:
An intricate, silk pavilion (let us say)
Open to the sky beside the sea, the Dome
Of a recollected soul, rigged with mysterious knots
Beneath the heavy wheel and rain-
Mill of the sexual hurricane, to be its capitol;
Or else it is an elaborate, sheltering house
Exalted stone on stone above an uninhabitable
Promontory of the main sceptic thought,
Wherein there wanders like a walking music through the rooms,
The suave singers of the lost story of love:

                                   as in my dream
A solitary worker, a methodical grim slave—toiling upon
A fraying reef or narrow purgatorial dike of sand
Extended from horizon to horizon, wearing away
North and South between two seas, one black and horrible,
The other light—carries without ceasing day or night
Dark water of the Eastern ocean and pours it from
A greased sieve into the bright bay.

                           Mother of death!
To see what the mind sees dazzles the material eye.
And the whole
Body is an Orphic explanation by a most eloquent spirit
Failing to be clear, who thus talks on and on until
Out of breath—
As one might say, "These are the faeces of an ancient soul"
(Pointing to the ground). But as for *me*, what shall I think?
—One thought comes to mind,

                    a great question,

                            and is lost;
And then another—also a great question—and is lost,

Appearing and disappearing out of the sad loops and errors
Of their wandering like human-headed birds. Vainly they
Call
Whom no man answers, and pass in disappointment away. But in
The shadow of their absence brightens like a monstrous gauge
The profane music
Of the Millennium. —The poet affronts the scarcity of fame

And names the age.

DUST

(Ars Poetica)

This is Spring for the last time. And poetry
Is dead—as when the Great Mind of the world,
Or the mind in fact of the one man or woman
Among us who can speak, has suppressed a momentous
Theme and nothing comes to mind in its place
And nothing is heard and nothing is seen
And the field is empty. Or it is like
An old ballad written down, or foot prints
Under the ice of time: the trace of one
Foot fall and in that print another print
Of foot falling and perished in the air.
(And thus began the motive of our endless
Patience—the waiting for the sound a thousand years
Of the one foot fall and to hear it again,
To hear it is the reason of our art
By which the greatest poet makes the deepest silence
In the empty heart of the strongest song.)
But in earth remained the writing of the path
Of two—human, or partly human—who were
Walking on a bare flat plane at the dark hour
The far mountain threw down this dust. Now read
The story of the day or night the far
Mountain threw down the dust, and the two wrote
And wrote (the one following the other across
The plain) until they were home. And then lay
Down in one another's arms, and the dust
Covered them and the hot rains sealed the scroll
With the seven seals of oblivion.
In time the fires of the mountain cooled.
And a lens of ice began the gathering of
This light by which we read (the two of us)
Which is now a large light, a love of light,
As one might follow with the eyes alone

The words of a song that was written down,
Already written under the ice of time,
An ancient path across a bare flat plain,
Our sentence, to the end. —What mercy of heaven,
Then, has sent these signs of the slaughtered dead
To unknot the tongue? There are so many unlaid
Ghosts in the world. Surely one among them,
Not yet inconsolable, will let us hear
(A young one who is still patient with us
And eagerly descants upon the momentous theme)
A sound of foot fall—human or partly human—
Out of the empty heart of the long forgotten
Composing the silence of the strongest song:
"Always like a new husband await the night,
And like a bride the rising of the light,"
Who wakens and walks out into the field
After a dream haunted by weeping animals
To find the patient spider has been brilliantly
At work and left a web articulate with dew,
Like mind a fragile theater of light,
A consolation to all of us who breathe
(And some, perhaps, of those who have no breath)
This Spring for the last time, the footfall of
Summer, long awaited, passing toward our death.

II

from
The Woman on the Bridge
over the Chicago River
(1979)

THE WOMAN ON THE BRIDGE
OVER THE CHICAGO RIVER

Stars are tears falling with light inside.
In the moon, they say, is a sea of tears.
It is well known that the wind weeps.
The lapse of all streams is a form of weeping,
And the heaving swell of the sea.

        Cormorants
Weep from the cliffs;
The gnat weeps crossing the air of a room;
And a moth weeps in the eye of the lamp.
Each leaf is a soul in tears.

       Roses weep
In the dawn light. Each tear of the rose
Is like a lens. Around the roses the garden
Weeps in a thousand particular voices.
Under earth the bones weep, and the old tears
And new mingle without difference.
A million years does not take off the freshness
Of the calling.

     Eternity and Time
Grieve incessantly in one another's arms.
Being weeps, and Nothing weeps, in the same
Night-tent, averted,
Yet mingling sad breaths. And from all ideas
Hot tears irrepressible.

      In a corner
Of the same tent a small boy in a coat
Sobs and sobs,

      while under the Atlantic

Depth and Darkness grieve among the fountains,
And the fountains weep out the grieving sea.

O listen, the steam engines shunt and switch
Asleep in their grieving. A sad family
In the next house over shifts mournfully
About staining the dim blind. The boy looks up
As the grieving sound of his own begetting
Keeps on,
And his willow mother mars her mirror
Of the lake with tears.

       It is cold and snowing
And the snow is falling into the river.
On the bridge, lit by the white shadow of
The Wrigley building,
A small woman wrapped in an old blue coat
Staggers to the rail weeping.

        As I remember,
The same boy passes, announcing the fame
Of tears, calling out the terms
In a clear way, translating to the long
Dim human avenue.

THE ROOM

A man is sitting in a room made quiet by him.
Outside, the August wind is turning the leaves of its book.
The door is open, everything is disclosed, each leaf, all
    the voices.

The man is resting from the making of the quiet in which he sits.
The floor is swept, his books are laid aside open, his eyes
    are open.
All the leaves and voices are outside in the restless wind.

Soon he will rise, or take up a book, or someone will enter;
Or, perhaps, a leaf will come in across the threshold, or a voice
Will blunder through the room, blind and unanswerable on its
    way elsewhere.

But now the room is quiet as the man has made it.
Everything in its place is at rest inside the room.
And the man is at rest, seeing each leaf, and hearing all
    the voices.

THE BOOK OF FATHER DUST

for Louis, my father

As God knows,

        the child sees,

                in the middle age
The strewn windfall of the befallen.

              Today
I am reading the poems written when
I was a child (the cobalt tower text
Of Hart Crane; spinster Stevens' intricate
Book of needles; oracular Yeats,
Unkind). And I am writing a poem
(It *must* be this one) conceived when I
Was conceived—

        a war in the world wind.

   . . . .

I am from Louis, my father—the dust.

   . . . .

In the middle age,

        the child sees,

                like an immortal,
His own begetting—the one shadow, and the faint

Sexual nuance of blown seed in the plumed
Shadow
Forty years ago—

                              this season, this hour,
This minute . . .

What was small is now large, what was young is
Now old, what was is now no thing.

                    .   .   .   .

                                        —How did the
Dead soldiers, as they arose in the dark,
Put on their shoes? That is what they did, when
I was a child; they arose
And put on their shoes, somehow; and walked into
Their graves.

                    But I came on as far as this
Bright morning, when all the gifts of the lineage
Were set down, as from
A spectral truck or vast galleon, warped
Silently in, out of the infinite, circling, high
Oceanic roads—
Great boxes on the paving,

                              the cargo;

                                        scraped,
Burned, shattered, crazed, torn, shaken—dust.

                    .   .   .   .

Amid the strewn befallen (this still
Morning of outcome)

                I marry Louis,
My author—the dust.
I take the dry yellow rubberband from
Around his wallet,

             and wind it on my
Book (in which
Will yet be bound by love in one volume
The scattered leaves of the whole world).

We are dust, Louis, and these are the lines,
God knows,

        which I must mend—
Conceived when I was conceived

               (bear with me)
At Xmas Lake,

      a war in the wind.

BY THE POOL

Every dwelling is a desolate hill.
Every hill is a desolate dwelling.

The trees toss their branches in the dark air,
Each tree after its kind, and each kind after
Its own way. The wind tosses the branches
Of the trees in the dark air. The swimming
Pool is troubled by the wind, and the swimmers.

Even though this is not a tower, this is
Also a tower.

     Even though you are not
A watchman, you are also a watchman.

Even though the night has not yet come,
The night has come.

THE RUNNER

The man was thinking about his mother
And about the moon.

            It was a mild night.
He was running under the stars. The moon
Had not risen,

           but he did not doubt it would
Rise as he ran.

           Small things crossed the road
Or turned uneasily on it. His mother
Was far away, like a cloud on a mountain
With rainy breasts. The man was not a runner
But he ran with strength.

           After a while, the moon
Did rise among the undiminished stars,
And he read as he ran the stone night-scripture
Of the moon by its own light.

           Then his mother
Came and ran beside him, smelling of rain;
And they ran on all night, together,
Like a man and his shadow.

THE FIELD, HER PLEASURE

Thunder over the field, voices
Of Memory, memory of the voices
And of thunder, thunder of memory
Over the field, slow after-speaking
To the lightning bolt, burdened
Interpreter of the quick, bright
Scratch.

          And then the following
Spirit of the crepuscular
Small rain.

          There is a man still
Sitting at the field's edge. The rain
Touches him here and there. And he
Sees her pleasure. It is rainy
Green. The lightning writes upon it,
And then the thunder in its time
Offers a meaning.

             But the rain is
A kingdom with its own god
Over which the thunder batters
Like the "ach, ach" of strange dogs,
And birdsong rises from the grasses.

The man owes the field a name—
Perhaps, "Her Pleasure."
Behind him is the house where she
Is but the field is her pleasure.
In the field are the graves of strangers—
Who are the strangers buried in
The field of her pleasure?

                    In the dark
Field is a green stream,
A sort of track that with the fainter
Mazy tracks of other streams
Leads down to a standing pond
And the one willow.

                    Out of the fascination
Of her eye, he sees at last the green
Court of her whole love.

                    At the pond's
Edge she is there—
With a long pole, in the dawn light
Pulling the sunfish up.

A SNOWY WALK

I

The tongue grows looser, the terms of praise
Slower, more inexact,

                     the day darker,
The rock cold—
And all the high terms of the wooing fallen
In a falling, a cadence.
I look backward
At you, my City of the Plain,
Iniquitous Sodom

                  wife of some years,
As on a snowy path you walk toward the woods,
On the darker side

                 where there is no sun,
And the snow breathes on your cheek,
The left,
Distance and intimacy growing together.

II

Seeing the beloved, first among fountains,
Then in the eelgrass

                 at the wide shore;
In childbed, also a wide shore;
On a snowy path—

Seeing what the light gives, and darkness takes away,
Salt seizes my eye.

III

I would be famous in your fields;
In your forests

            acknowledged
Huntsman;
In your deep lakes, rich gardens
Greeted by name;

               on your bright air
Unstream my banners—
Upon your snows, permitted pioneer.

PAT'S POEM

Semper dum vivam tui meminero —Erasmus, *De Copia Verborum*

This is a poem for my old nurse Pat—
Who had something wrong with her heart.

                                            Pat had
An old mother with a tongue like a cow,
With whom I slept.
And she had a father, out of sight, named John
Who died slowly in a back bedroom
Like an abandoned wagon rotting in
A low wet pasture.

                             Pat had a boyfriend
Whose best song was, "The Trail of the Lonesome Pine"
And a brother, Vince, who went to the war
Leaving a chained hound in the barn that howled
Four years straight night and day.

Most things Pat taught me were not true. What she
Did have a knack for,
Like skipping stones far out on the Lagoon,
I never could pick up. I don't know
What became of her . . .

                             Pat, failed nurse
With a too small heart, with all-consuming
Shadowy love I loved whatever
Behind that constant uniform of official
Imposture your freckled body was.

                                 First teacher,
Out in Denver or wherever marriage
Or the grave has swarmed over your hiding,
I'll tell the world that I remember

Every nuance of your plain brown hair
In Summer light.

                    Because of you I cannot
Tie good knots.
Because of you, I weep at marching bands
Because of you, I cannot depart
From any shallow friend, tell truth, keep measure
Or make an end . . .

                    So I talk on to you—
And on and on—all through the sleepless
Afternoon, as a child might to a stain
Upon a shade.
When will you come to wake me, Pat. Oh, when?
The long room darkens, and your poem's made.

            .   .   .   .

Out of the disturbed house, always below,
Robed as in summer curtains, sheer and white—
The dog's howl stopped, the confounded knot tight—
Comes up the stair dark, silence, and the years.
Semper dum vivam tui meminero.
All my life long I will remember you.

TWO WATERS

I remember two waters. One leaf-brown
From the sink pump, soft, for washing not drink.
The other, clear, one pail a whole day's
Good light.

The brown water was rain, on dark days and
Windy nights of its own weight down fallen
On roof, or driven against wall,

                            sunk then
To cistern dark and darkened among leaves,
Heaved up by the hand pump to wash a man's
Dark hair—and thrown out like fluent grief
On the sheep-bitten funereal home field.

The other water they sent me out for,
Each staggering pailful like a great lens
Raised to a great light,

                       hard water, for drink.
No grief or ease in it, as I think now—
Unhindered brightness of the deep-stored snow.

THE LOSS OF THE BELOVED COMPANION

Take away death, the last enemy—; and my own flesh shall
be my dear friend throughout eternity. —Augustine

Watching myself,

            naked,

                  in the mirror—;
My penis thickens, erect. For what? It
Is the mind bleeding through the body
Into the light.

          The picture of my body
Raises my prick—
A stupid connoisseur—who thus salutes the
Image of his lack,

              reduced by half,

                      trans-
Posed.

        Where will it end? They cannot meet.
Even as my helping hand arrives, it dies—

"Where are the objects of desire? The sheath,
The cradle, urn, and chalice of my sword,
My infancy, my ashes, and my wine?"

Thus, I stand (in a sense) quoting my own
Lines—; forging my signature to end the
Kindermord,

         weak flag of the seed's stream
Left in the void field,

               the uncollected,
Early work of my right hand—

                 "This is not
Solitude peopled by phantoms,
Imagined things to which some good adheres;
But, rather, critical vacancy
In which desire wells, as from a sourceless fountain
And spills itself into a cloudy basin."

. . . .

Watching myself—,

           impotent—,

               in the void
Mirror of my early art, it comes to this—
Sex and imagination are one.
Only the flesh (Hear me, now, father dust,
I have begun to speak),

           only the flesh
Is painted with our likeness.

             The gravity
Of the human image draws the heavy
Genital like an unseen earth—

             (O that it
Could once *want* to disclose itself,
Touch itself, hold it-
Self open)

   —the mother-awesome, absence-
Narrow, passion-targeted, answering,
Empty X

"Living in my desire I feel the anxiety
Of endless fall. . . ."

   . . . .

Naked—;

   in the mirrors of these lines, my
Soul salutes
Our death, the hero flesh, dear, darker, dying
Elder friend,

   and blameless *hetairos*—,

      doomed
Charioteer who takes in hand the great
Engine of hope, and in my armor drives—
Cursing—under the
Mountainous, chill shadow of the citadel. . . .

What can a man say?

     rising now, alone, starting
The lineage of the left hand (I speak
To you in verse, so that when you hear me
You will *not* die),

    forging my own will
(It is enough) in the silver light—.
I shall say more.

AFTER REPETITION

At once, illustrious Hektor took from his head the helmet,
and laid it all-shining on the ground. —*Iliad* VI

To place a poem among these poems
Without darkening the scene of
Placing the poem—

                 walking how lightly
To keep my foot from extinguishing the
Path, like a philosopher
Who makes his mind the only picture—
Not the mere poet broken in the
Saltmill of the manifest (the sea saying,
The shattering rock shore making it true)
But the mature
The self-determined maker

                         the *yogin*

                               whose walking
Lightly is a way—
Each good line a lineament—to make
More sure

            the slow overcoming of in-
Credulity

          the welcoming.

Leave mother and father to one another.
Leave off depicting. Avenge no one. Open

Your arms
             (when what I intended at first was
Only "The wind is in the house," and "The wind

Changes the place of light things")

        to his coming

                  by the way opened
(The undarkened scene, the windless bridal
House serene)—undisguising

                    setting down the
Battle mask
The plumed death's-head of nature on the ground.

(The image is death. Put off the image.)

The child shrieks

        as the gap displays

            his beauty.

THE BALLAD OF THE BONE BOAT

I dreamed I sailed alone
In a long boat, a white bone;
Like a strong thought, or a right name
The sail had no seam.

The mast, and its shadow on the sea,
Fled like one high lonely tree
Bent with the weight of the wind-fruit sown
By the cold storm.

It was a dream of dignity
When I steered on that plated sea
With a seamless sail, and a boat like a bone,
In a fair time of the moon.

There was no rudder in the long bone boat,
The compass was a stone—
The air was empty of the deep sea gull,
And gone was the cry of the loon.

The sea and the sky were one dark thing,
The eye and the hand as cold.
Unbound was my hair, unbound was my dress;
Nothing beckoned or called

But the words of a song
That had death in its tune
And death in its changes and close—
A song which I sang in the eye of the moon,
And a secret name that I chose.

And this is the song: "Straight is the way
When the compass is a stone,
And the sail has no seam, and the boat is a bone,

And the mast is bent like a tree that bears
The wind-fruit of the moon."

And now I sing, O come with me,
And be at last alone;
For straight is the way in the dream of the boat
That is a long white bone.

O GREAT O NORTH CLOUD

Friend of long standing, the wind-shaken rose,
   The shingle raised up and writhen like a back-
      Blown wing, our whole house of friendship
         A vessel twenty years at sea, the sea

Itself, graces and torn powers, and beasts under it,
   Far shores and delicate grasses great and small
      Risen as if summoned by a unique spasm of the moon . . .

It is mid-afternoon of the last Summer month
   And the children are calling to others a long way off.
      The seed has taken hold, and the seedsman has returned
         With his long knife, his team, and his great wain.

The sullen wasp is winding up his hive.
   All but the latest flowers are in bloom.
      Friend of long standing, the wind-shaken rose
         Knocks and will not be tied,

And a great cloud rises, northward of many lights,
   Like a dark stone upheld. O great, O north cloud, speak!
      "Winter," it says. "Winter, winter, winter."

NIGHTMARE

In the dark bottom of his head there lay
A severed head.

            He saw it when he closed
His eyes to sleep. And when he opened them
It lingered on things like a stain.

                He paused
To find a moderate term for what he saw—:
Things among themselves at first seemed
Quietly known to one another, and then
For no reason he could understand, flung
Themselves across the singular abyss
In shreds—burned and died to be perceived by him,
Standing a moment on the balcony.

In short, he saw that everything he saw
Was broken.

          And then the night formed whole
With all its stars about the man discovering
The brokenness of things.

            After a while
He went down to the street, and walked along
An embowered path.

              Someone who had been sitting
On a bench since sunset stirred impatiently
As if to rise as he approached him
In the early morning light. But the two
Men turned away from one another. They were
Like swans which avoid touching
Like the species of swans which does not touch.

THE LADY OF VILLA MALCONTENTA
DEPARTS WITH THE DAWN LIGHT

Tell the king, the fair wrought hall has fallen to the ground. No longer
has Phoebus a house, nor a prophetic laurel, nor a spring that speaks.
The water of speech is quenched. —The last utterance of the Delphic
oracle in reply to a question of Julian the Apostate

In the debates of the child who failed to thrive
With the boy struck by lightning,
Over which the bandaged man ("necrosis of the face")
Presides, does poetry enter in?

                         O, no.
The doctor at night, not hearing the first birds,
The gray faced mother-doctor
In the silence of not hearing the pain-song
Plucks a hair from the child's lip.

                       In the corner
By the mirror, the grieving mother-doctor,
Audience of all song,
Caresses her breasts and says, "Nothing is enough."

The lost face of the man without a face appears
And disappears in the corners of the mirror.
The mother-doctor caresses her breasts, and then
Wearily opens and closes her blond braid,
Averted from the flickering revenant.

"Agnes," says the struck boy, "from being
Much too much drawn up my penis aches.
Agnes, my heart stopped, out of your keeping."
Thus, on the limb of darkness, at the edge
Of the great space of the room, the struck boy
Empties his left hand of the argument,

And his right hand remembers its lost uses—
How taken up, how moved.

                        Where is the voice
The mother-doctor loves? The voice of
The master of the voices,
Toward which she would look round, did look, uncovering
The mirrors, stood up laughing, laughed, taking
Her hair down, shaking out the pins. It would
Say, "Beatrice," if her name was Beatrice,
"Apollo's house is fallen."

The bandaged man whose face was taken away
Concludes the sessions, "Pain does not heap up
Even where it most abounds."

                        A wind shakes him
And Dawn falls into the great hall. "Master,"
He says, "It is so long, and long. . . ."
The damaged ones murmur along the limb of
Darkness, like stormed fruit.

For a moment, at first light, nobody wants
The grieving mother-doctor. There is no one
Alive, or dead, or being born in the
Great dream house. For a moment, she has vanished
On the blond arm of the stranger, leaving
A slight discoloration in the rainy light—
"Perpetua, . . . petua, . . . tua, . . . tua,
. . . tua"—and cruel unwriting in the air.

THE THRUSH RELINQUISHED

One night there was no moon, and never had been.
In the space where the moon was

                                  the weather
Stopped, everything happened for
The first time.

                   I cannot imagine space
As it then was, the cradle unrocking
In the tideless air.
The man stopped, the shadow vanished,
There was nothing to read.

In their yellow groves the midnight villas
Went dark, as if the timid sleepers put
Out the fear lights, the dark being no more
"The dark." Patience in me ceased to betray
Itself by tears.

The poet is dead, and from his stare released
The stars weary of dance divest themselves
Of countenance.

                    No poetry tonight. Death tonight.
The thrush relinquished, my hand is in the open.
I can see every way.

VICTORY

There is a radiance about the bed,
From which I turn to take account of the
Radiance, the still space of the bed.

The household is filled with unborn children
(Some will be born. Some will not be born.)
Chattering on the stairs in the two languages
Of the born and the unborn. I sleep reading
The bright day backward like a Hebrew book.

Today, I saw the whole body of ocean
From a hill. First I looked away. Then I
Looked, and there it was.

              The children were playing
On the rocks. There was a woman I knew
Down there. Then I saw the whole ocean,
And we were no more scattered
Like swallows, or flowing from the broken
Hill like shards, but the swallows as they were
Before the scattering.

             I love you more.

The bed is a mountain, and the light is
The magnanimity of the mountain,
In the still space of the room where I sleep.
On the mountain we met a young hunter
Who asked the way of us, and did not wait
But strode off without the answer in another
Direction.—We climbed the iced flume
Carrying the answer to the grim rage

Of the top, where the whole earth stands, in the
Peril of high seeing—bed and abyss:

Birth bed, and sex bed, night storm bed of the
River dream, death bed of the born (despair
Of the unborn). I have come up now
Into the cloudy stone, and I have seen the earth;
And I have seen the sea, in the magnanimity
Of mountain light.

                   From the summit voices
Seemed to come. But when we climbed up there,
Our beards frozen, eyes turned from the wind, we
Found no one, and I had this thought, "She will
Never come. Not to him, not to me—alone of men."

And so if I bind on Apollo's phylacteries
I do it now to tell the plain truth.
Come, I will stop this talking. That is what
This voice inside you I am saying means.
Let us draw the black ship down to the divine sea—
Set the purple sail to the great death winds
Of the South, and empty
Out of the burden of our singing, you and I.
This is the whole ocean. Also the end.
After the wind stops,

                   the sound of the wind.
In the still space of the bed, I dream
The poet died. He had great difficulty
Dying.
He was reading a book about dying.
And then he died.

              And the woman Victory
Unbound the strap from his forehead

And the other strap from his arm, and laid
Them by.

And then she rested from her triumphing.
She unbound her breasts, and she rested.

THE DEPARTMENT

Siste, viator

Bereaved of mind by a weird truck,
Our fraternal philosopher
To whom a Spring snow was mortal
Winter—a wild driver in the best
Of cases, on the margins of
Communicability—exchanged a bad
Appointment in New Hampshire
For a grave in the Jewish Cemetery
In Waltham, Massachusetts. Across
The street from the University
And nine feet from Philip Rahv
He keeps his hours, perished
With little fame.

                          His name was Boime.

"A very heavy business, Grossman"
He would have said,
If he had heard his own death going
The way it did.

                    Immortality
Was our Summer debate. But in the snow's
Confusion blurring definitions
Darkened into mortal blows. Consider
The wit
Of circumstance which made that mind—alive
Unwriting, and naive—
Record its own demise on paper

As a flat brain wave.

                    Who speaks for
Boime for whom
The University found just this much
Room?

            His subject was the violence
Of mind, and the duplicity of his kind.
There was a wound, he thought, deeper
Than doubt where love

                            could enter, or
Look out—
Weary of the faithless civil compromise.
But that was not the wound of which he died.
He was a lousy driver who got caught.

An idle woman looked out on his burial
From her window
In the salmon colored house—

                                a disharmonious fact
Between the cemetery and South Street—
Sitting on a bed.
Nothing can be said, except

                            the passionate
Theorist is dead. In death he was
Unclear—

His aged father, like a gouged up root;
The bitter wife; the child of five
Who wondered how his dad would ever
Get out of that box alive;
The bearded bandits who cranked him down

Know as much as I do,

                    or anyone.

He left his work unfinished. Whether
It was good or bad nobody knows—
It was not done.

              Somebody is digging
On your grave, dear Boime,
Who in that snowfall, when you died,
Was farther South than you,
Better employed.

              Your name is
Penciled in now on a tinny bracket
By a casual hand. A baby
Has been buried at your side.

                    Since you
Died,
It is the second Spring,
And nobody has set up your stone.

                    God
God what a big
Thought, Boime, you carried into middle age—
Fat gladiator, treacherously caught
By a suffocating thin snow, chained
To a careening metal cage.

I am digging on your grave, like a starved
Dog burying a fact—

              If I say, "Boime, you

Were abstract,"

                         then with a great sweet
Smile, even from among the dead,
Who don't know anything, he will reply,
Leaning a little toward the Summer

                                        under
His unbalanced cloudy load,
And with his lovely gesture of the hand,
"Grossman, you do not understand
The place of theory.

                        Get off the road."

LAMENT FRAGMENT

Go down

(Forsaking the lagoons of bridged Atlantis)

To the mid-Atlantic ridge

               where are the crazed
Magnetic fields and roped sheets, and stains
(The disordered fabric of the volcanic
Bed chamber) and the gigantic vermicular
Testimonies

        and stare upon the great
Principle of the solid world—the original
Torment trace.

        Go down, for down is the way,
And grapple one stone syllable
Of all that frozen love's discourse
Onto an iron dredge

        and on it rise
(Borne on the enormous weight of its desire
For light and the air)

        until it explodes
Upon the deck amid the astonished crew.

Then empty out the nets disposed about
Your person, and fill them with the pieces
Of that one vast syllable

        and carry them

To Cahokia in East Saint Louis, where
My father was born who is dying now
(He was an honest man—mute as stone)

Place them on the top of Monk's Mound

(Go you. I am his son. I have no words.)

                                    and let

Them off like a siren.

THE LECTURE

Place a man in the center, and he becomes
The man who has prepared for a lifetime
To answer, and now is ready.

                        Sometimes,
There are trees at the edge of the clearing,
More often a sea. He talks on and on.
And his voice is carried up by the thermals
At the sea's edge, or down among the dark
Anfractuous trees, and the textile moss.
The lesson is staggering, and the examples
Come to hand like sheaves in a great harvest.

But, in fact, there are no trees, there is no sea,
And the center is some eccentric region
Of a bed or a room, and the question
Is the half-demented glance of a child,
Or a blurred silence on the telephone,
For which the man who has prepared a lifetime
Is ready.

        But the harvest is a great harvest.

After a long time, the voice of the man
Stops. It was good to talk on and on.
He rises. And the sea or forest becomes
A level way reaching to night and the thunder.

But, in fact, there is no night. There is
No thunder

III

from
Of the Great House
(1982)

OF THE GREAT HOUSE

In a dream to wander to some place where may be heard the complaints
of all the miserable on earth. —Hawthorne, *The American Notebooks*

I. To the poets

Let let let let be

                to the poets

                         praise,
And shame.

            To the sighted singer, in a
Passionate, laboring house. Praise!

                      But
To the blind singers among sleepy harvesters,—
Everlasting shame. . . .

              •   •   •

Of the great house I have in mind I dwell in,
The world,

At night in the Night Room, hung with the stars;
By day in the Day Room, with the high doors;
A Winter Room, where storms continually wreck;
The Summer Kitchen, my death-room set apart,
Where stands a black stone written on,

                              "Establish.
Establish rest. Establish rest profound,"

Hunting, lifelong—
The only thing that is, from room to room

· · ·

Everyone must write a book of mother, and
Father;

      but who could imagine how lonely
In their cold beds Louis and Beatrice are
Searching the chronicle of old memory,
By the secret lamp of pain?

                —Now, Beatrice
Is dying; and the great house fades with her
Fading mind; and her children are without
Hope,
A whole nation

          on its knees

            in the high
Courtyard, where the Fountain of the Arts is dry
As the sky above darkens, and shrinks—a grim
Page of which the sense is lost,

              where the dear
Names, like birds of the air, devour one another
In the dark. . . .

· · ·

—I stood in the Avenue, and vowed

               this book
Of mother and father against our vanishing—
As before in childhood

          I stood at curbside
Of the summer road, and saw: What was it?
One seed with its plumes. What was it within

The plumes? One plume, and the threads of it.
One thread, and the thread's tip.

                             Mother Beatrice,
Give me a very distinct cry.

                                 There is
No singing without a woman who wants
An answer sufficient to her injury—
Such is the Muse. . . .

Hear it, father Louis! This harp is struck
By a hand,

          a great harp, for

                  the nation:

              ●   ●   ●

Beautiful poems, like flowers! Beautiful
Poems—like webs, like seas working, like
Wind webbing black water blown flat with gray

Flowers of the foam. Beautiful poems risen
Against the granite cliffs in waves, exploding
The flinty shingle upward through the high

Window of the tower light. Beautiful poems
That I vowed, darkening the world,
Thronging the Avenue with the sweet sanity

Of profound tone, blind beautiful poems—
My servant animals, hunting the object of
Desire equal to mind's desire of an object—

Ringing and ringing through the midnight house,
Like an harassing phone call: Who is there?
Breathings only; and, behind that, the obscure

City of perpetual cry, whose citizens are
All mute, all dying, all enraged—
Beautiful poems. Beautiful, beautiful poems.

II. The dream of rescue

Lighter out enormous anchors to the svelte
Dutch warships, each ship with its swarm of ghosts
And signals

   the wind molests

      in the shelterless
Offing—like unmoored planets, painted less
And less by the sheer, exalted stormlight of
Distance

   (Too far, O planetary, too far
From the sun),

     one anchor with all its cables to
Each dark lighter, whelmed to streaming gunnels
By the horned iron

    Hope,

      as in the dream
Of rescue;—and no rescue!

      Lighter out
Enormous anchors, where the slender mothers are
Luffed there upwind; and all unscarfed labor

Into the wrecking storm, each

                                  with her whole heart
Of grieving.
And the strayed lashings, like tear-wet locks, escaped
In loops, and ray-like cometary whips,
Betray the

             torn skirts of

                   her vast secrecy
To the unsheltering light, and grief-song imperial—
Commanding tasks, impossible to perform . . .
Undesirable to complete. . . .

                         Whence the
Burden of this life,

                 the charter of this perilous
Cry;
As upward from beneath, toward the sea-bird
With a thousand voices—ocean's dove
Of long mourning—

                 a giant sea-beast, like
A drowned shield rises.

                 —But the truth is this
Is a picture—the mothers in irons in the
Unsheltering storm, the sun throwing down gold.

Night and day it stands before me, in the
Place of what I know.

III. The throat of the hourglass

On behalf of the sadness of men and boys,
Sing on the hills the

                    long deferred poem of
The third dimension. Sing on the hills, Shepherd!
While the universal grasses sound, a bass
Pipe of vast bourdon, the note

                           of the world—:
As from the throat of an hourglass, the voice
That remembers
A man who has no horizon,

                      the hero
Whose language is a heart, the strong heart
Of a bridegroom, who runs in the sun's brightness—
Wide-eyed, thinking. . . .

           •   •   •

                        —The night is the studio
Of my art. In the Night Room, the immense
Air of the void opens, and closes my book.

I am not entirely human,

                      writing in
Stony wind, and watry fire,
Pressing the strong heart of night's song against
The broken heart of mortal Hyacinth:

Beneath the life that appears—greatly beautiful,
Greatly cruel—is the life that does not appear
The poem makes appear,

Outered from the throat of the hourglass, that
Cries the bridegroom with beating heart to
Sentient rest—

      loved body,

            found in starlight,
The wide-traveling starlight, with all its eyes.

      •   •   •

On behalf of the sadness of men and boys
Sing on the hills

      the shepherd song,

            as of
White-flowering trees, attacked by running fire
Flowering transparent in full sun, blowing like
Birthstorm backward upwind, against the trees
In their flowering, flamelike flowers blackened
By the flowing flame—

      and left for us to see;
As when

      rowing across a lake (Beatrice was
In the boat, and I was rowing) against
The distance,

      unvanquishable tide, I heard
The bass note of the waves, like grassy wind;
And saw the universal sky

      of this
Dusk page, by the pain-lamp of a low sun—

As through the maelstrom throat of the hourglass,
The torrent of the image,
This poem of my love, pours out on you.

IV. At the shore

And, then, he put the cup into her hand
—Quick, vine-scribbled,

        silver, chalice of

                offering—
With perfect luck, as the hand that is ready
Does see of itself

      the goddess is there,
Athene amidst her honoring for it
Has never ceased, beside the holy sea,
Night or day—;
The old man, Nestorian, habitual as the sun
And moon,
Across the gray foam-flowered threshold of
The Seen

    greeted the

        viewless, the gray-eyed:
Addressed the deep Unseen,
In the onlooking of ancestors,

          —knowing
Every grief is a person.
Praise! Though she came in the rags of our body,
He put the cup into her hand. . . .

And, then, he took the Past, Louis; and the Passing,
With quick hands;

                    and What Is To Come! and made
A loaf for the good day

                  —beautiful poem.
Cast wet and dry of worlds in a green bowl:
Water of the air, and some salt of ocean;
And bright sands of the field, in its ebb season,
The reaping

        of a gold

              reading of earth
In the good sense of the mill, and

                  poured in
Seething the green yeast that lives forever, but
Flowers in our world, the

            power of rising
—and his hand struck the difference of these,
Like the strings of a harp, into one lovely skin:

           •   •   •

. . . The question is at ease on a sunny stone
In the great Sabbath heat that makes it fit—.
This is my body to which the wonders come,

Beautiful poem, sweet mixture; and the truce of
All the strings. Louis, as the lamp brightens, the
Chronicle will show a whole nation sings

I imagine you.

        —There is a storm on the beach.

In truth, it is like my world after all;
But there is enough. Beautiful poem where

There is enough. Everyone has a body. Look!
At eighty, suddenly it was discovered Louis
Wished to be held in arms. Beautiful poem

Of a very old man in the nurse's arms.
Rest, reliable spirit. We are so little human—
So stony, so water-like, who built the great

House at the gray shore.

                              —But this is the last
Age of silence; and, God willing, the first of
The unmistakable voices to which we say, "Yes, you."

Rest, rest, reliable spirit, frail and light.
The waves sing three syllables, woe-man-grief.
The mothers take you in, except they die.

Beautiful poems. Beautiful, beautiful poems. . . .

V. The only thing that is

From room to room, my servant animals
These songs, her body, lifelong have led me
Hunting the object of desire equal
To the mind's desire of an object

                              —dancing,
As thinking is, a dead one holding the left
Hand, and a dead one holding the right hand,
Whose left hand holds another living hand:
No living hand holds

                    a living hand in
The dead dance on mind's cold mountains, or
Through the rooms of the great house at the shore.

                ●   ●   ●

In truth, it is raining. There is no moon.
And the thunder comes: the restless daughter
Of a restless mother, casting away worlds—
Mother of a restless son.

                    First, I saw
The acetylene signal, across the ocean far away,
The lightning with its white, white hieroglyph
"Let be,"

            rip-tooth of the birthstorm;

                            and heard
Beatrice, following in thunder, from childbed
Rise with all her scars, casting away worlds.

                ●   ●   ●

Let me tell you how the thunder grew,
And seemed mingled with familiar women's voices;
Sirens entered, then,

                    and in rain were lost,
Or overtaken by the unmistakable word-
Streak of birthcry;
And the white, white lightning—wounds as they are
Known to God—
Inscribed one stroke on the black stone above.

Now, there is nothing in place of what
I know,

       the only thing that is—

                     the world
With winds and rivers.
The house is first a torch, and then a ruin,
And then a sweetening field, quiet after storm.
Songs flower in the night by whose light we dance
And go up.

THE SLAVE

And the angel of the Lord was by the threshingplace
of Araunah the Jebusite.   —*II Sam. XXIV, 16*

I

Why must the poet rage?

                                    Because of nations,
And the angels.—With my right hand I turn,
And turn the pages; and with my left hand note
This place.

                    Read, angels, if you can; and say
To the nations (Jerusalem, first of all)
The poet has sent a sign,

                                    a light blue
Romanza, the eloquence of water,
The sound of a girl talking with her friends.

I have come a long way to work out this:

II

—My left hand and right hand are not the same.

By contrast to my right hand, my left hand
Is clearly older, more worn.

                                    My right hand
Seems innocent beside that other one—
Less, or differently, used; certainly,

More vulnerable.

(By the bad light of
Evening, at Jerusalem, in the blind heat
Of a June *sharav,* two glasses of pure
Water are infinitely differentiable.)

Witness the scythe-shaped scar—right index finger:
Witness the damaged nail of my right thumb.

This happened, as I now see, because my
Right hand held what my left hand worked upon,
And received the wounds.

Witness, also, the scar
In the pad at the base of my right thumb.

III

Nonetheless, my left hand is closer to death.
You can see in this half-
Light—the lines in the left palm make a mortal
M, a *morte.*

(Outside, under the flail-stone
And hot swingle of the iniquitous farmer,
Jerusalem, on the high threshing rock
The meticulous South wind sifts and sorts.
"Only this is," it says. "And this other
Is not anything.")

My right hand, despite the
Scars, is really asleep (but I do not
Know how to wake it);

and deep in my brain

Left and right hand are like two glasses of
Very pure water on a day when two
Glasses are enough.

The lines in the palm
Of my right hand form an X—no letter.

IV

Perhaps, that is why my left hand does this
Writing, or why when reading I lay my
Left hand on the page, and with my right hand
I support my head.

Outside, in the wild
Night, anyone who looks can see the floating
Islands of cloud darken the Via Dolorosa
And moonlit Gesthemane,

and carry a cool
Moment over the Mount to Bethany—
But at this season no rain.

The wind blows
Down my lamp; and it explodes on the floor.

This is the breaking up of the *sharav*.

V

Now, behold! A struck moon among the high
Grecian islands of shade—conscious scripture
Without letter;

and hear! The sinister farmer
At work in the lower dark—battering, battering:
"This is, and that other is not anything."

(Outside, the West wind is like a very beautiful
Girl, her two breasts

                              glasses of pure water,
The right slightly fuller than the left, as
She raises her left hand to adjust her hair.)

The sun rises behind the Dormition—where
Mary fell asleep—like lilies in full hands.

What is the beautiful girl doing now?

                                        She is
Talking to her friends, a very beautiful girl
Who today will wear blue for the hot weather.

VI

Every nation has an angel. Most are pale;
And stand in their killing clothes night and day.

The angel of Jerusalem is pale,

                              and stands
At the highest pinnacle of the threshing
Rock teaching curses to the sinister farmer,
Jerusalem,

                    as the sun rises. The wind shifts to
The South, and begins to sort the night's threshing,
"This to life, and this other to the fire."

I do not study with the aim of saying
Trivial things.—If the angel of Jerusalem
Had human eyes. . .

               If Jerusalem were a pool
Where a very beautiful girl might walk or sit,
As she pleased, or bathe. . . . If the angel of
Jerusalem had ears for the light blue eloquence
of water. . . .

               But Jerusalem is a slave.
My left hand signs—"Death"; the right makes its mark.

BOW SPIRIT

stanzas on the pathos of our generated life

But tell me of your lineage, for you are not come from a famous
oak tree, or stones.   —*Odyssey* XIX

I

Blind bow spirit,

               my mother,

                               Beatrice
This poem in the likeness of a countenance

                    (the eyes, the nose, the brow,
The wen upon the brow, the august beard,
The mouth never right—

                   never right) saying
What can a man
Say who has not yet begun to speak—?

Damn you Beatrice, who took my voice—mother.
I might be anyone.

              One line materializes
(It is October, and the air is dry.)

And then another
(Wait. Something will come to mind. Wait. It will.)—

The wild blue aster.

II

Hoi. On the mountain

           the dark cattle

                              (on
The blind breast of the mountain in the death-
Winds of October)

                are driven from the
Upland pasture with blows. Hoi. Light.

                            —The boat
Is upon the water, the harbor and the
Harbor islands shine

(The beard is for the resurrection. Louis
Hates it,

           the wen upon the brow, and the
Knotted mouth).

              There comes to light

(October is a deep, deep lake in which
The mountain is seen,

              and the cattle)

                    a face
Like the reflection of a sky
(Does Louis have a face? Does crazy Bea?)—

Hoi. How long ago the blaze was

                      (the marriage)
That blackened all my other histories.

III

In mountainous

       October

              at the high
Lunar noon, terror
For the children came over me suddenly,
As I lay hiding my hands.

Suppose (mother of the grasses)

                 for all the
Talk no man has spoken
And now he begins, setting all the poems
To one side—;
What would he say, if the trying and not
Succeeding were to end

           and his opened
Mouth

    (tears streaming down his face, as linnet-
Like the lines weave

          of sere flax the sheer
Facial shroud)—?

        Come in, children. Come in
Now. It's going to rain.

IV

This poem in

       the likeness

              of a countenance
Saying what a man can who has begun
(Mother, have you ever seen a man's face?)
—If he spoke you would not hear.

                     If you heard,
He could not endure your tears.

               (Allen, I

Have never loved anyone.)

             If he survived

Your tears

       then he would live forever,

                  awake
Listening to your tears. . . .

That is how I came to this damned line-work
Straying among the stones, Louis, and the
Chanting oaks, my mother Bea;

             among death-
Winds on the mountain
Fighting with sleep, with cold erections, bent
Over my book

(Lying down is overwhelming)—

Writing now with flat square hands, my
Ghastly wen, the beard, and this
Flowing mouth.

        I do not love you,

                        mother.
Die where you will.

V

Unteachable Beatrice,

                my death-ship

                                spirit
Imagine now the panache of a master
Walking with his hand on hip—

                              carrying
A man's house of staring into the forest;
And then out into the sun.

                       So my eyes
Which fed a million years on flickering
Minerals

           (Louis's small eyes, my father's)

Are born in the grave bright air drawn up from
This cold October well of air.

                      Let be
Mother—

         Let this light be

                  that is.

VI

Everyone has a face, a blowing shroud,
A sheer wealth of furnishing, a sailing
Gaze and lineage, like a torn net

                            descending
From the forest primeval, from the earliest
Ages of the world.

                    (All-focusing like a
Lens her sex, bow spirit,
Is the leader

            inter urinas et faeces
The beautiful roads)

               —The lineage descends,
From the mountain down, by the mountain path

(Forty years unable to concentrate
My mind)

           past the reeking gibbet, and the
Harrowed sidehill field, to the sullen valley
Stream

       (Louis is alive still but mad)

                   and out
Into the dazzling estuary, and the air

O this blue aster is an autumn, a dry-
Wood flower,

          a wild flower

              of the Fall.

VII

Thus diverse lines meet

                      and knot—one line and
Another (the eyes, the wen upon the
Brow, the august beard).

                      The road into the
Dark is first a road into a dark place

(This is the hour, mother, to marry your child—)

And then the carrying of the gaze out
Of the rainy dark

                    into the brightness of
The sun. Look! A wind of a sort

                          a whispering
Messenger (bow spirit)—

                island

                  calling

To island in the shine

A LITTLE SLEEP

I

Lying on my right side, I see the wall.

Lying on my left side, I see the window.

Facing the wall, lying on my right side
(Easing the ache in my left arm), I see
As in a dream the same wall closer to
My eyes.

        Facing the window (lying on my hurt
Left arm again), I see the garden beyond
The window, almost out of sight above
My eyes. Looking at the window, I am
Affronted by the opaque light concealing
Everything, except a few branches high up.

Turning once again onto the ache in
My right arm, I see the white wall flaking
To older red underneath,

                and remember
The branches high up, now behind my back.

II

Facing the wall, my right hand reaches the
Bed's head, which is a dark high cloud of wood
Reticulated downward in windy scrolls,
And my right foot touches the bed's cold foot.

My right cheek lies, almost without sensation,
On the sheet.

By pressing with my left foot
Against the bed's foot, I can make the ache
Less in my right shoulder. But my erect
Penis (lying this way) is jammed between
My belly and the bed's grave underworld
To the point of pain.

            The whole bed hangs cloudlike
Above the floor.

            To my left is the wall
Like an erased Book of the Dead. To my
Right is a window high up, shallowest
Of eyes.

        The bed's head is above my head,
And beneath my feet is the bed's cold foot.

III

The bed stands between the wall and window.

On the bed lies a shadowy boy who must
Be consoled,

            and also a man who must
Believe the consolation, which should be
A sentence he can say that the boy can
Understand.

            The boy is the man when young,
And I am the man now, remembering the
Branches high up, perhaps with wind in them.
There seems so much to say about the few
Branches,

            which might be anywhere, in this

Or another time, seen through the affront
Of light by this man or boy,

                        lying in
The ache of his left side (weary of much
Turning) who remembers the visionary blank
White wall, flaking to red, so near his eyes.

IV

Turning to the window (my penis is
Easier now, but my right shoulder is cold)
I feel more like sleep.

                    Seeing the branches
High up in this or another time, the
Shadowy boy stares at the branches, his
Mouth swollen with hunger, his penis aching,
His right shoulder cold.

                    Lying on my left
Side my left hand reaches to warm my right
Shoulder, and my right hand holds my penis, or
(Very gently) the boy's. The light batters
The branches.

                    We sleep a little, and sleeping
The same branches appear with a steady wind
In them.

                 In my right hand his penis grows
Less troubled. Reaching my left hand into
The shadow under his left shoulder I warm
His right shoulder, together with my own.

I say nothing. A little sleep is good.

V

As I turn again onto my right side

The shadowy boy turns with me, pressing
His penis between my legs, and his pained
Mouth (very gently) against my neck.

                              Waking
Now I see before my eyes, on the erased
Death-page of the blank wall, the shadows of
The high branches which are behind my back,
In the inscribing light.

                    The ache in my
Right arm starts. The dream was like the waking,
After a little sleep.

                    My cold left shoulder
Warmed by my right hand, I face the shadowy
Blank white wall flaking to the older red,
Which was the color this room was before

I made it ready, and lay down to stare—

The bed's cold foot beneath my feet, and
Above my head the high bed's dark cloud head.

VI

Getting up (rising on my right elbow,
And twitching the blue quilt behind me with
My left hand, standing, etc.) is more complex
Than I can explain.

                    The garden appears,
Level to my eyes, with paths severely

Indicated by the light.

                The dear shadow
Has vanished, or dispersed into the disturbed
Bed between the great head and the chill foot.
Now, *you* console him. Warm him in your arms
As I have done. Kiss his penis, and his
Pained mouth now addressed to you.

                          I can go
Either to the right, or left,

                  seeing or
Remembering the garden with branching
Paths, and the visionary page erased,
Or faintly inscribed

(White over red, shadow over the white)
By a strengthless, hasty, obsessive hand.

THE PROTHANATÏON OF A CHARIOTEER

David Zil'berman
(born Odessa, 1938—died Waltham, Mass., 1977)

Le combat spirituel est aussi brutal que le bataille d'hommes; mais la
vision de la justice est le plaisir de Dieu seul.   —*Rimbaud*

I

It was as if

                something had slipped from me,
Down a sharp stair—;

                    as I waked from a short
Dirty sleep in a low chair

                 in August
Burdened with my dream of phantom Zil'berman
Dead at just this void time of year,

                    and now
Reposing

        through his *jahrzeit*

                  in the frescoed
Chamber of a cheap coffin (the lid was
Cracked, and let in light), wearing a gay pair
Of striped pants bought for him in Chicago
By his wife,

           in the Jewish cemetery
In Waltham, Massachusetts—near the fence . . .

Did this really happen?

               Was David here?
A far cry from Odessa where he was born,
Or the high Turkman desert of Kara Kum
Where, as a Sanskrit weatherman, he learned
That he,

           perhaps alone of men, would finish
In happiness the work begun,

                 being the
Thirty-fourth incarnation of Śankara,
A Hindu sage, whose parents chose to have
One wonder son of merit who would live
To no great age;

           but not (my God!) that he
Would have his skull crushed by an adolescent
In a stolen car

(The terms of spiritual combat are obscure)

         as he returned at
Evening, on his bicycle, from an untimely
Seminar;—

And, having nothing in his pockets, die
Unidentified, and thus

           be houseled by
A priest, buried a Jew,

           and mourned a bitter
Husband, and a haunting friend (intimate
Alien with transparent hands),

                    the father
Of some girls

          (quite absent-minded now), also
Mysterious philosopher, the one
Perhaps who *knew*. . . .

                    II

                    And so it was as if
Something slipped from me irretrievably
Down a sharp stair to a phosphoric sea,
Waking me from my low chair—.

                         In humid August,
Drenched with Caspian air,

                    the unsown graveyard
Was scattered everywhere with tiny, yellow
Flowers, a sort of dust—

                    intricate, five-petaled,
Nameless, gay.

               I raised a yellow flower to
My eye,
And all the petals fell away,

                         either because
The flower was wild, or else it was mid-
Afternoon, and late in the life of flowers
That live one day . . .

                    "There is no picture
Without an artist," David used to say,

"But the artist without a picture is
Divinely free."

           I cannot hear the voice
Of holy Zil'berman. It had no tone.

And when he talked, he wandered around the room.

III

The graveyard is on the right of South
Street, as you go down from the University
Toward Main.

           I used to see him walking home,
But on the left side,

               as through a forest,
Or beside a sea,
With his hand on hip, head up, like a guide

Or, like a charioteer walking beside
A vast chariot with a high chair, and mere
Streak of galactic wheels, so real I could
Not see,

         but with a sound that I could hear—

(Unless I only heard the roar of the
Boy in the fast car, coming on, that brushed
His handlebar, and made the catastrophe).

O, who would believe that as a man dies
Who knows nothing, or very little, so also
Dies the sage?

(Where were the marks, then, Summer weatherman?—
The high stable illusions of your golden
Colchis, where the white carp in rows suck like
Pigs at the bland teat of the warm littoral;
And the mariners steer by the bright mirage,
Steadier than our stars?)

                    Specific chapters of certain
Books will now lament inconsolably—
They have lost their understander forever:

The Structure of the Chariot, and also
The Book of the Aśvattha lift up un-
Intelligible voices

              (Now they are
Men of tears).

           The Modal Methodology—his
Pale mother, in her throes—has veiled her lips.
The tent has fallen of the Transcendental
Reduction, and weeps for David Zil'berman,
A man whole, with all his desires.

                  But the face
And the great eyes of Gregory Palamas
Signify, "Let there be silence. . . . The Lineage
Does not provide a Holy Man to die
By violence."

IV

          He has gone down like a doomed
Bride to the low tower of his fate

                unknown;
And like the sea sound at the bottom of a stair

Yellow with the phosphor that sleeks the stone
The road roars above the frescoed chamber of
His shattered head

               (the world that *can* appear—
In which these words are read, the faint traces
Of disabled care).

             The guide is dead

                  who used
To make his way through Waltham, as in a dream:
And now I sometimes do the same.

                  —Veda reader
Zil'berman, drowned Argonaut
Of our humid August of the awe and dust,
And ghost

       it was a graceless sort of teaching
To get thus lost,

            unless you have become
The truth you taught, the unapparent end
Of seeking—

(We did not kill you; nor did the boy in the car.)

     born to disappear.

V

O charioteer,

Release me from the burden of this speaking.
I am overcome by sleep once more,

a mere

Singer in a low chair with the one key

—"Hear me, Allen. Death is nothing you must fear."

That only scars the door.

Release me, David.

—"Hear me, Allen. Death is nothing you must fear."

Release me.

"Death is"

from the burden of the

"Nothing you must"

speaking

"fear . . ."

This is

The Prothanation of a Charioteer.

SENTINEL YELLOWWOODS

(Yellowwood—*Cladrastis lutea*)

Sweet sweet sentinel yellowwoods *lutea lutea*
Guarding my track morning and evening, and gracing the air
With odors and blossoms to the left on the side-hill
And the right near the wall. Sweet sweet the one and the other.
Seven years not seeing them, seven seeing them but not
Knowing a name for them, and seven years naming them too.
Sweet sweet sentinels *lutea lutea Cladrastis lutea*
Odorous silent adorning lutes.

                Now and then, how full
The world is. Look at the yellowwoods! Look at them
Lion-like watching the way, in the morning to work and
At evening to this kind of singing

Lion-like waiting all the more patiently now I have
Named them, come into the strength I can render account
Of the beautiful way I am not always sad.

                    Sweet sweet
The shadow of yellowwoods, even in autumn, even at
Evening. I am going to die soon, and their shadow foretells it
Enlarging the world.

        I can see it without me.

                  Under the
Yellowwoods, the one and her brother, lion and lioness
Together without me, bereave me, bereave
Me as leaf-like my body.

      •   •   •

If I do not look up as I pass, then they call to me
Sweet, and I stop and turn round and go back and stand still,
Breathing the fragrance. What was I thinking of? *Lutea*
Lutea, thinking my thinking I did not look up, and often
They called to the air, to the children, and nobody heard the
Sweet sweet

                    —like a sleeper who

                              sleeps on into the sunlight
In a bed closed by curtains a family of women skillful
And comely sitting in sunlight embroider with birds that no one
Has seen, but only the women the widows and daughters neat
Fingers of sunlight with loving attention,

                              imagining glorious
Birds and the flowers Arabian, and blazing with gladdening metals
Mysterious flies

              sleeps on into the sunlight, in the dark
Of his dream. And he does not see the wind billows the fustian.

                    •   •   •

Do the yellowwoods suffer, the sentinel yellowwoods, in autumn
In winter do they starve on the shore of the sky?

                              At the gateway
Of evening, of lion-blond autumn, leonine death-gold of autumn
Adorning, the answer does come, in splendor of lutesong
Arising within me:

              the soul is alone

                    —like the flowers of
Yellowwoods, *lutea lutea,* white pendant clusters sucked by the bees,

White fragrant gusts of milky spring rain.

                                    I call to them, calling
Their call, the two lions, the call that they raise in me
Morning and evening, my words of their teaching: the soul is alone.
—Sweet sweet sentinels *lutea lutea Cladrastis lutea!*
Seven years not seeing them, seven seeing them but not
Knowing a name for them, and seven years naming them too—
The fragrance of flowers arising within me, sweet sweet
Breast-perfume seized by the mind.

                                    Now it is winter, and the fustian
Of the leaves, that fine work of the sun, the winter wind draws
Back to the earth. But the sleeper is awake, and gone down
Singing his lutesong
This crooked path into the world and out.

AN INVENTORY OF DESTRUCTIONS

Be it life or death, we crave only reality. —*Thoreau*

Non fui. I was not.

             Fui. I was.

                       Non sum.
I am not. . . . *Non desidero.* I do not care.

          •   •   •

Nothing has occurred to me, except my life—

It is a book much used, for many years marked and adorned;
By hard turning stained with spittle and tears;
Trusted body-slave of my treacherous hands—
A cold, stubborn, lonely soul—a great house of dreams . . .
Closed, it is the picture of the whole mystery
Laid bare, night with all the stars. Opened,
An empty bed with one brown stain.

                            In the
Book at hand is a book beyond all hands,
As the sky is in a well . . .

Ascend to the sky. Drink of the water there.
Take it deeply to heart—as a tree in
Hard rain is beaten into ancient metal
By the first green waters of love.

                      Honour that book,
The inventory of our destructions.

          •   •   •

Non fui. I was not.

           —The door of the room
Of mother and father had a glass handle.
In the early morning the corridor was dark.
On the left,

         the wide doors of the linen closet,
Ajar, poured out odors of the wet earth
From the cool, dark-folded flanks of new sheets—
Damp sexual bodies at samite rest, deep
In shadowy pools of their own mysterious
Patience. On the right,

            the flowing well of the stair
Drew up windy, thin, leaf-stained, watry light
Disclosing at the center of the door's
Glittering knob—many diamonded lens—the one
Unreachable, silver nail . . .

               ●   ●   ●

           Fui. I was.

                —God does not
Permit the poet to continue. Others may
Continue. But the poet must not continue.
For the poet is the governor of the nation,
And God speaks first to the governor, and
Lays His rod on him:

         "The truth of the poem
Dies when the virtue of the nation for which
It is the poem dies. To establish
Zion in Palestine is a failure of
The imagination.

       Establish rest!

The angels of the nations are pale voids
Of the imagination. Zion is pale.
The great house is not to be established
On divisible earth.

Establish rest profound."

Deep in the brain's cave is the world set right,
A great house, vocal, intelligent, alight.

* * *

Non sum.
I am not.

—Look!

Everywhere in earth and heaven
Are graves. Some are very small, and are silent.
Others speak. A man listens among the graves
Where the willow's windy shadow, the daylight's widow,
Flicks and flicks her idle noose against a stone.

(It is the hour she does her killing in.)

Through the diamond lens of the air he stares
At the one stone,

and the trees are filled with the voices
Of the unborn, their wistful backward language.
So, the poet speaks to the unborn in the
Language of the born, and to the born he speaks
The language of the unborn.

—Break down and build!
Destructions are of the poet. Death is of God.

"Whenever the children take their turn at the music
The sorrows do not correctly move in the figure.
Honey of the bright day stains the tragic note,
Griefs falter on the stairs, and there is more
Light than the high windows of the right tune
Can measure. . . ."

      •   •   •

Non desidero. I do not care.
—No page is more beautiful than the fields.

Praise to the poet of the fields, and of the
Hedges between the fields which make a path
Toward the river in whose mouth is Paradise.
If this world were a body I should never
Be alone until death . . .

    —The greatest poet
Laid the fields down upon the unsown earth
In accord with the idea of the fields
As it is known in the mind of the lineage
Which is a turning tree left in the field
For shade and for music.

    Rest in the shade of the
Tree which is the lineage of the poet.

My father is Louis. Beatrice is my mother.
This is my picture.

    —In a dream Beatrice's
House was thronged with bodies which weighed on me
—white and unfeatured—revolving in blind
Eddies and dry storms. The doors of the house
Were open. And I looked about with a hard stare
Saying,

"I will throw myself down from a
High place, and wake." But God said,

                                       "Continue!
Continue the stony book of your life."

                •   •   •

God gives one stone.

IV

---

from
*The Bright Nails
Scattered on
the Ground*
(1986)

THE SONG OF THE LORD

There is a table bountifully spread.

In the full sunlight when there is no cloud
And under cloudy skies,
And when there are no stars and when the stars
Distill the time,

                the table stands in a field.
It is late morning and the service shines.
The guests have wandered from the company.
The Lord is alone.

              It is good to hear
The voice of the Lord at rest in his solitude.

The guests have wandered from the table set,

But they hear the voice of the Lord at rest:

The song of the Lord in solitude goes up,
Ten times enfolded, blue, and saturate
With law to the heavens at noon of gaze,
And down among the graves and the darker animals.
The song of the Lord indicates the dust
Of the roadway, the random hammer of the sea,
The riddled vase of mind and mind's dependencies

And pain lost otherwise and lost in this.

The voice of the Lord opens the gates of day.
Air streams through our eyes and brushes the pupils

Streams through our eyes and this is how we see.

THE WORK

A great light is the man who knows the woman he loves

A great light is the woman who knows the man she loves

And carries the light into room after room arousing
The sleepers and looking hard into the face of each
And then sends them asleep again with a kiss
Or a whole night of love

        and goes on and on until
The man and woman who carry the great lights of the
Knowledge of the one lover enter the room

          toward which
Their light is sent and fit the one and the other torch
In a high candelabrum and there is such light
That children leap up

       unless the sea swallow them
In the crossing or hatred or war against which do not
Pray only but be vigilant and set your hand to the work.

THE GATE

The day shrieks open—like an ancient gate,
Turning on a bronze post, socketed in stone.
And then shrieks shut, turning in the same
Stone. And the dead bolt of the dark is shot.
Someway from the gate, at the edge of a road,
Is an oak. On the road men and women pass,
Carrying things, leading animals.
Above the road, the oak tree hangs out one
Fear branch, heavy and black. There is no city.
Only the gate, the road, the night, the oak
Tormented by the weight of its one limb,
And men and women carrying this and that,
Leading animals. In the day the men
And women see many things. . . .
At night the men and women see one thing.

What do the men and women see by day?
They look down, and they see the road they walk.
Whether they walk toward the gate or away,
Or linger in the light, they see the road.
When they look at one another, they see
The one body of each of them that stands,
As it were, in the open gate of light.
There is no city of light, only light.
The fear-branch of the oak casts down its shadow
In the road they walk, as if it fell
All day into the dark.

At night, the men and women of the road
Look up. They all look up, in the dark,
And see the sky.

They have set down the things they carried.
The animals sleep in the road at their feet.
They do not remember the gate. They do
Not prophesy the light. They see one thing:
The sky, the sky, the sky, the sky, the sky.

A SHORT WALK

alma Venus —Lucretius

Standing in the road and nobody calling,
After morning rain, and before the rains
Of April noon and April afternoon
And evening. On my right, is the house where
I live. On my left, is the house where
I do not live. The road behind I have
Gone over, and the road before I have
Also gone over, and above is nothing,
And beneath my feet is the earth. —A destruction

Has befallen here among depthless pools.

It is equal whether I stay or go.
Nobody is calling. I can hear sounds,
But they are not calling: there are birds—
The birds of April—but they do not call;
And the winds departing that left the early rain
I hear, and the winds approaching with the rains
Of noon and April afternoon; and the sound
Of the one thing that can happen on this earth
Gathering to take effect . . .

What am I doing now? I begin the walking.

Here are white flakes, veined ash—I think—driven down
From the cold tower of ash, the flowering dogwood,
Luminous ruin. Nearby, loiters the cherry tree,
A sleepy shepherd with his flute in hand strayed
From the meadow, adorned with flowers of his song.
Alma, alma, is it a dream? Is it
Even a dream? The being that has gone through
All its growth—neither the wise (tower
Of ash) nor the beautiful!

In the daybook, mark this day for a *feria*—

A destruction has set me free. I hear my voice
Say, "No!"—the first truth. I can hardly move
The leaden cape of the air. On the right,
At the turning—a sill of death, the silent
Drawing into vacancy. That way
Everything is bright because it is falling,
Brighter than diamond, than wedding stone.
The left is my way to the human end,
The open, whither no one is calling.

Where the open is, there the festival

Never falters on the shores of the sky.
I rose from my chair, hearing no calling,
And walked out on the rain-wet road, and turned
At the drawing of the diamond stone,
And threw off the leaden cape of the air. . . .
To the greater poet remains the song!
The being that has gone through all its growth
Neither the wise, nor yet the beautiful.
For the phoebe was heard again this year

In April but did not nest in the garden.

—Only a few things happen to a man,
And he does not know another thing. But
They are what he knows for sure. It is like
A short walk to the human end alone, seeing
The one thing that can happen on this earth,
And hearing the rain of April afternoon
Come on, and the midsummer rains. And then
The rains of Autumn and the coming of the snow.
And then—*alma, alma*—the poem of the snow.

AT THE SHORE

On the *plage* the mothers make paper flowers,
And the children buy them with North Sea shells.

What do the children do with the paper flowers
The mothers make? They plant them in the sand

And the North Sea wave waters them with storms.
Who rests assured

              in the house of the senses?
It is all restless turning and vanishing.

Dreams tire the mind, exhaust the heart of
The sleepers—many dreams.

                  Therefore I say
To you up there who are not in this with me
You who do not know me except for this,
The man or woman awakens exhausted
At the heart.

          I cannot imagine the dead
In ecstasy. I do often imagine
The dead in torment,

             and the blue dome of
The house where the order is written.

THE PATIENCE OF THE DARKER LOVER

Though we have had many days, this is the first night of our love.
And we have loved and slept some, and I have dreamed:

                                                   Even in your arms
A darker lover drew my sex away toward cavernous infoldings,
And fear and shame awoke in me because I did not love you
But was devoted to that other one,
More radical, more severe, who was waiting for me in the place
I'd searched for thirty years ago and not found then,
And yet still did wait
Until this first night of our union, this first sleep in your arms.
"I have waited a long time," she said. "Now come to me." And I went,
And you went with me, down into the city of the unlived past.
I said, "It is time to go, my sister, to the darker lover,
For she has waited a long time." And we went to her, you and I,
As if we were one soul in the one body,

                                    down into the city of the past
Which was not two cities, but the one city of the past we failed
To find before. On the first night of our love she took us—
The lover of the unloved body of my youth—as a woman takes a boy
And draws forth from him the deep first seed of his whole love;
And also the lover of the unloved body of your youth—as a woman
Takes a girl, opening the source of a stream which has never
Yet flowed, that no lover of your youth man or woman had opened.
And I thought, "In the darker lover we have found a stronger bond,
Because she has waited a long time in the city of my unlived past
For me, and in the city of your unlived past for you.

                                        In one another's
Arms we have gone back, in middle age, and found her on the first night
Of our love." And now I wake, and find *you* in your cotton gown.

THE STARE

The whole world cannot comfort you—

Not the visible world extending its ringed hands
And gazing into your eyes like the sun at noon,
Capable lover, or sun at five o'clock,
The husband returning who kisses your face
And in the dark night shows you all his thought;

And not the invisible world that breathes
Quietly on your swollen lips at dawn
And offers you its perfect breasts to suck.
Desire that is greater than the world stares
From your eyes,

                and I am acquainted with
The earth's rage when women look at the mountains,
And say to one another, "Not enough, not enough,
We will not sleep in this place"—ignorant
What can and cannot be,
And how each thing has a deep-set boundary mark.

—What is left? The work of common life
And long familiarity discovers love.
Do you not see that drops of water falling
On stone after a while penetrate the stone?

The machine of the world will stop, and there
Will be nothing but rain of the *primordia.*

And nothing is indifferent to our claims.

THE LOCK

Outside the long window of the final poem
—The final poem, like an empty room,

                                            a high
Room of state
Where burns the last of the perpetual fires:
A guttering tongue of the ancient flame,
Or mother-word of the unutterable name
Faltering
In a sealed air, in the night, and unknown weather—

A starved moth of a cry, a moth or cry
Of the soul, or soul

                            batters its wings

Against the transparent gate of the final room
—The dark room of the longest art where burns
Fame of the word that is mother of the cry
And desire of the heart,
The term or a form of the nurturing light
I am drawn to as by fate

Unsealed in a dream when I first remembered
To fly
And felt the lapse and glide and the strong sexual
Rising of sight,
And gazed upon the diminished fields of the world
Without fold or flower, as from the tower
Of an ecstasy. . .

Until night came down bearing laws
And I awoke,

              and saw far off through the black
The thin flame of the mother-word; and heard
The calling of a name
From the sealed mansion of the book—
The final poem and the adamantine lock.

EURYDICE, OR THE THIRD REICH OF DREAMS

Wir Gewaltsamen, wir währen länger.
Aber *wann*, in welchem aller Leben,
sind wir endlich offen und Empfänger.

We have the power, we last longer.
But *when*, in which one of all our lives,
Are we, finally, open and found?

—Rilke, *Die Sonette an Orpheus*, Zweiter Teil, 5.

Aëllo the wide woman with fish eyes
Is seated before the door of her house.
She is bright as dark is bright. Her hair
Is tied back. Her large breasts are concealed.
She does not wear black but white as white
Is black. I stand before her and she makes
Love to me. Her legs are closed but she
Draws me through her vagina into her womb.
She teaches me I do not know what . . .
She says, YOUR GUILT IS UNDENIABLE.

•

This is not to be sent.—I am calling you from so far. Please hear me under all
the noise. I am awake now. I want no more dreams tonight. Between my
bed, which fills almost the whole room, and the window is a small card table
at which I am writing to you, and a bookcase full of the weepiest books—
Das Dritte Reich des Traums by Charlotte Beradt, *Se ressaisir ou disparaître* by
Isaac Pugatsch, *Encore un effort* by General Robert Close, *The Black Book of
Prague* . . .

    —I had to stop for a little while. I have found one book here—
a new one—which enumerates each convoy from this city, every name and
the circumstances of death as they are known, the exact number of people
gassed on arrival—boys, girls, men, women—the number of people killed
later, and the survivors. Allen, it is one thing to argue from the point of view

of the living and rant and rave, but then there is the side of the faces in this book—the side of the dead!

                        I am sure there is also a book of my own death somewhere, but I do not know who has it. If you could find it, you would see that it is not like a poem or a letter—it is more like an August storm that blows up over the castle and the river, and fills the air of afternoon with sudden darkness and the plumed seeds of the cottonwoods and dust, and then passes over the city like waking or sleep. You would see that it has nothing to do with destructions, or with the beginning or the end.

                            •

—For who shall say, as between the man and the woman,
Which is the most delighted in love? Or as between
The new dead in the moment after death and the unborn
In the moment before birth, which is summoned to
The severest judgment? Or as between brother and brother,
Or sister and her sister, or a sister and her brother,
Or friend and dear friend, which will answer for both of them
And for the common world? Go and ask the flowers
Because thought is like the flowers, and of two kinds:
There are the flowers near to me that close in the night
—Such as the outlandish lily that is my particular
Passion, or the anemone—and make a holy difference
Between night and day, sisters confident of memory.
But other flowers keep open to the rains of the moon
Like men and women intending to be present at the inter-
Course of their own death—as the night-blooming *cereus*
That blossoms at the hour prophetic Job called pain,
And knows the profane horror of the millennium;
Or the common marigold—*souci des marais*—
Flower of the marshes raped night after night by the trained
Dogs of the torturer and the torturer's question.

                            •

My dearest, we have a duty *not to remain in the aftermath of things.*

I read just now, in Charlotte Beradt's book, of a doctor who dreamed—in 1934, after one year of life in the Third Reich—that the walls of his room had disappeared and as far as the eye could see no apartments had any walls. And then in his dream the doctor heard a voice on a loudspeaker, "According to the decree of the 17th of this month on the Abolition of Walls. . . ." I think it must be either Heaven *or Hell* where there are no walls!

—In the book of convoys, the new one I mentioned to you, are photos of children holding the hands of mothers and walking the same streets I walk, with sight of the familiar trolley in the background. In one picture is a young boy with an intelligent look who stares in a very serious way at the camera. Whether he *knows* something the others do not, of course I cannot tell . . .

•

But we are guided in these matters by
A spirit of our kind—whose eyes are averted,
Whose color is a blue of the bland mortal power,
A mother of light who gives us all her face
In whose domain we are—in love—unknown,
And subjects of the whitest languages
Wherein the light discourses generously
Of her children who have in her no name—
Translator snows.
Left to themselves all things tend toward this place,
A visionary dome, or Tivoli with stars inside
And one gigantic wheel, a *Rieserad*
On which the lighted coaches slowly turn. . . .
There was a night, my brother, when mother came
Wrapped in a mantle like a Summer storm,
After a ball, with sequins in her hair
And the outer air, and whispered to each of us,
"My dear"—though I was here, and you elsewhere
In another time. Help me to keep
Her holy, in whom we met.
The walls of the world have been abolished by decree—
It is the one new fact of history

That nothing is holy, now, because there is no place:
The pallid angels of the Nations in their killing clothes
Preside
With female courtesy at the abolition
Of the face;
And the trained dogs of the moon have slipped
The leash and hunt us through the *Buchenwald*
Or immemorial beech forest of the book
And all the fragrant paths lead to a lock.
By their nature men desire to know the end
And the beginning, and thus they violate
The nurseries of the snow. . . .
If you come for me, you must avert your eyes.
You must forget my body and my name,
Because I speak another language
In which nothing you can say is true, nothing the same.
There are no spirits and there cannot be—
Just the seeds of the world—and the flowing leaf—
Dropping one after one into the bed of the Spring.
—I write to you in English to be safe.

•

I have attempted to look away from the paper, and beyond the book of names and faces, in this room which is now very empty. I shall soon stop, and—because I have not gone mad with fear—try to sleep and try not to dream.

I want no dreams tonight. Last night I dreamt that posters had been set up on every corner proclaiming in white letters on a black background the twenty words people are not allowed to say. The first was "Lord." The last was "I." The others I cannot remember. But tonight, please, no dreams.

•

The strangest of my many bodies lies awake in the night.
Above me is a gate and in it the weary angel of the gate
—Emptiness of a body without the passion of the ghost,

The unbodied substance of him like cords blowing in another
     air—
Appointed to stand undying at a threadlike border as of
Another mind, where knowledge of the world comes to an end,
And thought comes to the end and stops. He holds two books:
With his thin left hand he shows me the book of the wound;
With his right, the book of the knife. At first the wound
Is beautiful like a new friend or an astonishing ornament.
But soon it becomes familiar and cruel with the cruelty
Of a frightened woman or a beaten child grown dark and
     cunning
With malice and secrecy. After that, it begins to speak sentences.
And, finally, it makes its mark. Thus, I finish reading in
The book of the wound and turned to my left side where the
     angel
Of the gate shows me the book of the knife—his voice like
A tree with wind in it, his whole body more and more the sub-
Stance of morning wind: "Now the knife works without the
     hand.
In the cities of man it works on the bodies of the citizens.
It works only on the flesh of men and women. It has no destiny
Toward wood or stone." He ceased and disappeared, leaving me
The two books of my life, the book of the wound and the other
Book of the knife. In the strangest of my many bodies I arise,
And cross the threadlike border of another mind, and wake.

                              •

Midnight here. I shall mail this letter in the morning with some misgiving.
What I feel is a new thing for me, rather passionless—neither anger, nor
resentment, nor painful love, a sense of the others as *so other* that only the
calmest affection is elicited, *a very white sort of compassion.*

                                        In Vienna once—in
the old days, after the war—I crossed over from the Lueger-Ring to Freud's
apartment at 19 Berggasse to see the famous *Abhandlungzimmer,* but it was
empty—all the images, and pain, and labor at thought and writing leaving
not even a stain in the air. Only light was left after all the destructions—

meticulous and absorbed—neither adding nor taking away.

But there was
the shadow of an old man lingering in the room, exhausted and appalled by
the realization that everything he knows is true, everything everybody
knows is true. . . . Why should I insist on love? Why should I *insist!*

•

Dearest, I am captive in a House where dark
Is light, governed by an inconsolable queen
With whom I am in love—Aëllo, hypnotic
Nurse. She teaches me the lure of the source,
And the terror of despotic memory.
If you do not come for me, I shall remain
Naked, her sexual slave, and eat dust.
She rules *all worlds that cannot be*—by force.
But if you *do* come—do not look at me—
Do not touch me—*do not say my name.* . . .

THE JEW'S DAUGHTER

If I have misunderstood *this,* I have mis-
Understood everything! —I say to you,
I have misunderstood it all. But I
Have not mistaken this misunderstanding,
Because I dreamed a true dream. This is
The dream:

                 —at the dark edge of a darker falls,
In the moment when the fall seems to stop,
The moment of recovery and transparence
Before it drops into the first abyss,
The first of many soundless cataracts,
Each under each, down which the world pours
Like rivers of water to the darkest dark

I enter a dream theater—the truth shop

Or *Wunderkammer* of our common life
In the transparence of the last blue wave.
It is a window, lighted from within
By the blue light of the last wave before
The fall, that draws my mind. Jews of the town,
A father and a mother and their one
Child who is a girl, keep the truth shop in
The clear light at the edge of the abyss.
Through them pours the grave waters of the falling
World—lustrous, relentless, cold, quick and still.

They have what I want.

                 —a leaf it is, or willow
Rib of a druid fan scribbled with runes,
The last piece of the story. It arouses me
Like a woman. —Then, burdened with the price,
I lean through a crease in the transparent stream

And pay into the hand of the girl my whole
Stake for the poet stick.

"Now *read,*" the girl said.

And I translated the words by the blue light
And thus diminished them. It was as if
Great, pilgrim birds—eagle and noble swan—
Sent to the world's center from the darkest limbs
Of earth had lost their way. And the one went
To the mountains, and the other to the deep
Lake of streams to sing and die. —Finally, in the
Theater of dream, I read out the plain words,
And heard the others, dead and unborn, or living
Still, reading the same words that concern us
Through all the time the words are true.

It was
The identical, birth-blue, starving cry
That worked back across the water to the ship
Of Thamus when he whispered to the shores
At windless Palodes:

GREAT PAN IS DEAD;

And heard answer him the oldest lamentations,
Not of one person but of many—mingled
With amazement—and not of persons only,
But even the strangled voices of the stones.

Death comes in waves (they cried). *Death comes over us*
In waves, as each day's light is a wave. And
The last wave falling plucks us from the shore.

These words are the dust, O daughter of the Jew.
(The sea is also dust) —This was the dream.

I *must* remember you.

TO THE TRUMPETS

Perhaps he built a throne—as you would place
A chair for a friend, in a particular light;
But no friend came that day. And so his preparations
Went on and on, becoming more filled with desire
And gold:—more tables of offering, more flags
Of Presence, more scepters of His power laid
Ready for His hand.

               It was all made from trash,
The refuse of government offices, in which he wrapped
Dead lightbulbs and used furniture salvaged,
Or bought. And he wrote prophetic announcements
In watery lavender, like Constantine
Who used no other color.

               I liken the brightness
Of what he made to the desire of the male
That builds up a golden throne for the greater
Poet to come, of whom we say: "Except
The one face there is nothing else." This is
The madness of great love.

               And great love
Changes all things. As once by the sea I went
Down—
The vast sea; and I heard the whole of it
Shift in its bed and rise toward me—grown
From all its throats, and from each throat a thousand
Particular voices, and each voice unanswerable;
And I saw the huge trunk of a dead tree,
Cut elsewhere and heaved up there. And I knew then
For myself—beyond the grim scavage of art—
The desolation of the world and ignorance
Of the heart.

Therefore, call Him the high *hetairos,*
And build up His throne—composed of lost things—
According to the ordinance of knops and flowers:
A chair for the lost one of lost things made,
An imperial friend who comes to sit
In the kingdom of our patience and the courtesy
Of our sexual gold. Hang out more flags,
More and more flags. . . .
Let there be more scepters of His power laid;
Inscribe more glyphs of announcement in watery
Lavender.
Hammer in more gold, more gold, more gold.—Summon

The school children to see what we have done;

But tell them nothing I have just now said.

STANZAS ON THE MOURNING OF NATIVITY

I

This June of inordinate rains what grows
Grows out of all measure.
The early season seems late so burdened
It is with leaves.
And the flow and lapse of streams, other years
Soft and slow,
Hews down *termini*. The mills dissolve
Into their race.
We are turned back—baffled, dispossessed—
By gigantic felicities
Of hedge, the long Spring grass, and trees.
Our sex has enlarged
The seeds of the earth. We have conceived
A child that must
Not live, because there is no dwelling in the wild
Fields of the world—
No tower, no law, no song, no animal—
He can inherit,
The woman sterile, the man of uncertain mind.

II

Such infants are like voices. The green trees
Are full of them.
They hold the sea islands. They have their nations
And their laws—their towers,
Songs, and animals. They are begotten too
Upon pictures, and also
In the cold false light of phosphorescence
On the bed of death—
At the moment of death when the visions come.
They are the hundred-armed,

The horned, the radiant, the too radiant children
That crowd the portals
And stairs, and from the infinite nursery of
The unborn look out,
Like light flashing from water as the wind rises
And the day cools—.
And somewhere deep is the long curve of a dark arm
That comforts them,
When night seizes the sea islands and the nations.

III

In middle age he will not be quite whole.
This will be known
By his hesitation between man and woman
And by the terror
Of his sympathies, as light which is a sufferer
Shudders and grows pale
To be whatever thing on suffering earth
It falls upon.
For every real there is a hundred of his kind.
When he says "pain"
It is your pain. When he says "shores of ocean"
Black headlands
Receive the sea blow after shocking blow.
Of passions that have
No place in the world something is always born.
—Is there among
The burdened trees obscured by their own leafage
One oak that towers
Above and is the tower of solitary nurture?

IV

Now in his infancy, where swaddling light circles
And twists its chains
And everything that lives lives under the law
Of light spectacular,
Emperor of the unborn, he keeps the nest
Among the exploits
And suffering of the light—fugitive, voluptuary
With black all-focusing
Religious eyes, the father of his father
Of uncertain mind,
And mother of the sterile woman who
Has lost her road.
When he looks up, the stars leave signifying
And turn their fires;
When he looks down into the pouring mirror
Of the wimpled flood
The fire that passes through him from the stars
Burns in the water
Like a serpent crowned, and bites the root.

V

We are turned back.—The earth has overlain
The seeds of earth,
And will not wake. The rains drive down the nest
That was so high.
And thus begins the mourning of nativity:
The father grieves
In the meadows for his fantastic child.
The barren mother
Wanders the wet roads. And for its infant lord
The light weeps
Like an animal. The Summer will come,
The river slowly

Draw the ignorant flood into the sea.
Nothing will be
Added, and nothing taken away.
—We are alone.
In the world of the unborn his poem is
Very long.
In the world of the born, it is what you see.

THE BROOM

Corruption is the reciprocal to Generation: and they two, are as Natures two terms or Boundaries. —Bacon, *Sylva*, 328

First, on his neuter instrument the child
Sucking and blowing casts out simple threads;
And, then, the boy his trumpet, the girl her silver flute
Adorns as with webs the first light after rain.
Then, the man and woman in their prime utter
The vocal song, companion of the sun.
And their song goes with him, circling the world—
Cold at the pole—hot at the equator—
Gone up with the gull—with the highest clouds—
Where Phaeton screamed, for there was too much light.
So much light was darkness and he came to harm.

I have seen the bright nails scattered on the ground.

• • •

We sleep where we can. But the best thing is
A high bed in a white room with a picture
Of a dark seacoast, and the sea in storm.
The floor of the room must rest on the face
Of the earth and not be lower or higher
Than the common road. If there is dust,
Then sweep the room. Here is a worn straw
Broom to rid the vestiges of the gods.
Give up your little light, and let it be
Dark of the first darkness—the dark that was
Before the lonely, lonely transgression
Of the stars. And beware the unextinguishable
Interest of dreams. . . .

Between the head and foot of the high bed
The grim genital of the world repeats

In you and says its say: The body is
The place of final claims.

                        Until the slow
Light fills—
To whatever honor—by whatever servile hand—
The long, Lethean chalice of the day.

                    •   •   •

Lying late like a false watchman
In bed at the hour when vigilance would
Be rewarded on the ramparts, and a thin
Snow falling like the pollen of desolate
Ashen flowers blowing above in the dark
Lunar garden of the winter sky at noon—
My death appeared to me high up in the air
Of a white room,
Like a snarled hank of somebody's black hair
—And more and more often now appears.

It convinces me I have seen my soul.

                            —Watchman,
As you walk the ramparts with the cold sift
Of the snow charging the shoulders of your coat,
Have you seen your death-soul as I have mine?

                    •   •   •

Whenas the brightest planet hunts the moon
As, now, night after night I see it do,
Sense falls like thin snow on broken ground:
If I loved you but not of your body,
I did not love you. But I loved you

And I love you.

THE PATH

The unborn. The unborn are what we were.

Among the unborn was one who saw the moon
In splendor rise. He was nearing the end
Of his life in the house of the unborn.
He knew it because the splendid moon had
Risen above the field. That was the sign
Of the end of one life.

                    —Then he harvested
The field in its season. Together with
The other harvesters he sang the song
That weeps for the grain.
Now the harvesters are a century gone
From the field

            and the neighborhood grows older.

So many of the children have grown up
The path is less distinct year after year.
Soon it will be hard to find the short way
Through the field to school.

                    —Orpheus, Orpheus,
Master of losses, the children are come
And gone,

            the harvesters.

                    And the trees return
With slow steps and the flowers with a skip,

And the grasses trailing long memories.

THE GUARDIAN

After a while, things go on of themselves.

(There is no comfort, but there is a guardian.)

The guardian is a man and a woman.
He stands. She rests her body on his body
In an easy confident way.
She does not touch him with her hands

                                        which hold,
Instead, objects signifying mysteries.
He also does not touch her with his hands.
Her left leg grips his waist and lies along
His thigh, opening her body to his sex.
Her right foot follows to the ground his left.
Beneath his penis struck into her cunt,
The smooth sack of heavy testicles hangs down.
And from the mountain altar of his hair
A human light descends on her. Her lips,
Curled back, display the long tooth of her love.

(The man and woman are in ecstasy.)

And this will be going on after my death,
And this will be going on after your death also.
But after a long time, all this will stop, flow
Back into the universe, cease form, cease
To be metal, become another thing,
Become nothing.

THE SOUND OF A VOICE IS
THE STORY OF ITSELF

The sound of a voice, telling of its love
In clear words to the man or woman for whom
The love is love of that man or woman,
Is the story of itself
As the world is the story of itself
Told once to each mortal listener who
Hears it in a room alone—
How the sun shines, and moon adds its syllable,
And winds their emphasis, and rocks of earth
The full stop of difference which makes the sense
That claims him for the lineage of the world,
"Mortal listener!"

         Mortal listener,
We have two breaths: the one that takes in
And is silent,
And the other one that gives, the outering
Breath and summoning of the world that tells
The story of the world.

         The first breath is
Infant and mute, the feeding breath. It takes
The element which is the same in trees,
And on the lake, and in this room and the next
Room where the others are,
Into the body over the human tongue asleep.
The voice falls silent then, and body feeds
On the vital substance of the alien air,
And is alone, and suffers its death when full
For it can be no more.

         But when the tongue
Awakes out of that lonely infancy
And turns to love,

A second breath that speaks makes of dead air,
And words common as air, a deathless summoning
Voice telling of its love
Which goes out at the punctual midnight
Of the body's dark, like a seed on the wind
Or a child leaving home,
And is never alone because it is
The sound of the world
Telling the story of itself in love
As to a woman bathing and making ready
Or a solitary man in a boat
Which the winds drive farther and farther
From the land.

And death will take us all, mortal listener,
At the sharp intaking of the deepest breath.
The sound of the voice falls silent; but then
Begins again telling the story of itself
In clear words: "This is love, which was your death,
And will be as you make it
Truth,
Between the one breath and the other breath."

QUIES, *OR REST*

A woman goes from room to room. She extinguishes
One light in each room. Darkness follows her
And in the last room she is overtaken.
Then, she mounts the dark stair confidently
And enters the room she sleeps in, and lies
Down in the dark, where a man in the dark wakes
A little and covers her with his arm.

New Directions Paperbooks—A Partial Listing

Walter Abish, *How German Is It.* NDP508.
John Allman, *Curve Away from Stillness.* NDP667.
Wayne Andrews, *The Surrealist Parade.* NDP689.
  Voltaire. NDP519.
David Antin, *Tuning.* NDP570.
G. Apollinaire, *Selected Writings.*† NDP310.
Jimmy S. Baca, *Martín & Meditations.*NDP648.
  Black Mesa Poems. NDP676.
Djuna Barnes, *Nightwood.* NDP98.
H.E. Bates, *Elephant's Nest . . .* NDP669.
  A Month by the Lake. NDP645.
  A Party for the Girls, NDP653.
Charles Baudelaire, *Flowers of Evil.* †NDP684.
  Paris Spleen. NDP294.
  Selected Flowers of Evil. †NDP71.
Bei Dao, *The August Sleepwalker.* NDP692.
  Waves. NDP693.
Gottfried Benn, *Primal Vision.* NDP322.
Carmel Bird, *Woodpecker Point,* NDP662.
R.P. Blackmur, *Studies in Henry James,* NDP552.
Wolfgang Borchert, *The Man Outside.* NDP319.
Johan Borgen, *Lillelord.* NDP531.
Jorge Luis Borges, *Labyrinths.* NDP186.
  Seven Nights. NDP576.
Kay Boyle, *Life Being the Best.* NDP654.
  Death of a Man. NDP670.
Buddha, *The Dhammapada.* NDP188.
M. Bulgakov, *Flight & Bliss.* NDP593.
  The Life of M. de Moliere. NDP601.
Frederick Busch, *Domestic Particulars.* NDP413.
Ernesto Cardenal, *Zero Hour.* NDP502.
Joyce Cary, *Mr. Johnson.* NDP657.
  Second Trilogy: Prisoner of Grace. NDP606; *Except
  The Lord.* NDP607; *Not Honour More.* NDP608.
Hayden Carruth, *Asphalt Georgics.* NDP591.
  Tell Me Again. . . . NDP677.
Louis-Ferdinand Céline,
  Death on the Installment Plan. NDP330.
  Journey to the End of the Night. NDP542.
Jean Cocteau, *The Holy Terrors.* NDP212.
Maurice Collis, *The Land of the Great Image.* NDP612.
Cid Corman, *Sun Rock Man.* NDP318.
Gregory Corso, *Long Live Man.* NDP127.
  The Happy Birthday of Death. NDP86.
Robert Creeley, *Memory Gardens.* NDP613.
  Windows. NDP687.
H.D. *Collected Poems.* NDP611.
  HERmione. NDP526.
  Selected Poems. NDP658.
  Tribute to Freud. NDP572.
Edward Dahlberg, *Because I Was Flesh.* NDP227.
Alain Daniélou, *The Way to the Labyrinth.* NDP634.
Osamu Dazai, *The Setting Sun.* NDP258.
  No Longer Human. NDP357.
Mme. de Lafayette, *The Princess of Cleves.* NDP660.
Robert Duncan, *Ground Work.* NDP571.
  Ground Work II: In the Dark, NDP647.
E. Dujardin, *We'll to The Woods No More.* NDP682.
Richard Eberhart, *The Long Reach.* NDP565.
Wm. Empson, *7 Types of Ambiguity.* NDP204.
Shusaku Endo, *Stained Glass Elegies.* NDP699.
Wm. Everson, *The Residual Years.* NDP263.
Gavin Ewart, *Selected Poems.* NDP655
Lawrence Ferlinghetti, *Endless Life.* NDP516.
  A Coney Island of the Mind. NDP74.
  European Poems & Transitions. NDP582
  Starting from San Francisco. NDP220.
  Wild Dreams of a New Beginning. NDP663.
Ronald Firbank, *Five Novels.* NDP581.
  Three More Novels. NDP614.
F. Scott Fitzgerald, *The Crack-up.* NDP54.
Gustave Flaubert, *Dictionary.* NDP230.
Gandhi, *Gandhi on Non-Violence.* NDP197.
Gary, Romain, *Promise at Dawn.* NDP635.
  The Life Before Us ("Madame Rosa"). NDP604.
Goethe, *Faust,* Part I. NDP70.
Henry Green, *Back.* NDP517
Allen Grossman, *The Bright Nails. . . .* NDP615.

Martin Grzimek, *Heartstop.* NDP583.
Guigonnat, Henri, *Daemon in Lithuania.* NDP592.
Lars Gustafsson, *The Death of a Beekeeper.* NDP523.
  Sigismund. NDP584.
  *The Stillness of the World Before Bach: New Sel.
  Poems.* NDP656.
John Hawkes, *Blood Oranges.* NDP338.
  The Cannibal. NDP123.
  Humors of Blood & Skin. NDP577.
  Second Skin. NDP146.
Samuel Hazo, *To Paris.* NDP512.
William Herrick, *Love and Terror.* NDP538.
  That's Life. NDP596.
Herman Hesse, *Siddhartha.* NDP65.
Paul Hoover, *The Novel.* NDP706.
Vicente Huidobro, *Selected Poetry.* NDP520.
C. Isherwood, *The Berlin Stories.* NDP134.
Ledo Ivo, *Snake's Nest.* NDP521.
Gustav Janouch, *Conversations with Kafka.* NDP313.
Alfred Jarry, *Ubu Roi.* NDP105.
Robinson Jeffers, *Cawdor and Medea.* NDP293.
B.S. Johnson, *Albert Angelo.* NDP628.
  House Mother Normal. NDP617.
James Joyce, *Stephen Hero.* NDP133.
Franz Kafka, *Amerika.* NDP117.
Bob Kaufman, *The Ancient Rain.* NDP514.
H. von Kleist, *Prince Friedrich.* NDP462.
Elaine Kraf, *The Princess of 72nd Street.* NDP494.
Shimpei Kusano, *Asking Myself. . . .* NDP566.
Jules Laforgue, *Moral Tales.* NDP594.
P. Lal, *Great Sanskrit Plays.* NDP142.
Tommaso Landolfi, *Gogol's Wife.* NDP155.
"Language" Poetries: An Anthology, NDP630.
Lautréamont, *Maldoror.* NDP207.
Irving Layton, *Selected Poems.* NDP431.
Christine Lehner, *Expecting.* NDP544.
Siegfried Lenz, *The German Lesson.* NDP618.
Denise Levertov, *Breathing the Water.* NDP640.
  Candles in Babylon. NDP533.
  Collected Earlier. NDP475.
  A Door in the Hive. NDP685.
  Light Up The Cave. NDP525.
  Poems 1960-1967. NDP549.
  Poems 1968-1972. NDP629.
Harry Levin, *James Joyce.* NDP87.
  Memories of the Moderns. NDP539.
Enrique Lihn, *The Dark Room.*† NDP542.
Clarice Lispector, *Soulstorm.* NDP671.
  Near to the Wild Heart. NDP698.
García Lorca, *Five Plays.* NDP232
  The Public & Play Without a Title. NDP561.
  Selected Poems.† NDP114
  Three Tragedies. NDP52.
Francisco G. Lorca, *In The Green Morning.* NDP610.
Michael McClure, *Fragments of Perseus.* NDP554.
  Selected Poems. NDP599.
Carson McCullers, *The Member of the Wedding.*
  (Playscript) NDP153.
Stéphane Mallarme,† *Selected Poetry and Prose.*
  NDP529.
Thomas Merton, *Asian Journal.* NDP394.
  New Seeds of Contemplation. ND337.
  Selected Poems. NDP85.
  Thomas Merton in Alaska. NDP652.
  The Way of Chuang Tzu. NDP276.
  The Wisdom of the Desert. NDP295.
  Zen and the Birds of Appetite. NDP261.
Henri Michaux, *A Barbarian in Asia.* NDP622.
  Selected Writings. NDP264.
Henry Miller, *The Air-Conditioned Nightmare.* NDP302.
  Big Sur & The Oranges. NDP161.
  The Colossus of Maroussi. NDP75.
  From Your Capricorn Friend. NDP568.
  The Smile at the Foot of the Ladder. NDP386.
  Stand Still Like the Hummingbird. NDP236.
  The Time of the Assassins. NDP115.
Y. Mishima, *Confessions of a Mask.* NDP253.
  Death in Midsummer. NDP215.

For complete listing request free catalog from
New Directions, 80 Eighth Avenue, New York 10011

†Bilingual

Frédéric Mistral, *The Memoirs.* NDP632.
Eugenio Montale, *It Depends.*† NDP507.
  Selected Poems.† NDP193.
Paul Morand, *Fancy Goods / Open All Night.* NDP567.
Vladimir Nabokov, *Nikolai Gogol.* NDP78.
  Laughter in the Dark. NDP470.
  The Real Life of Sebastian Knight. NDP432.
P. Neruda, *The Captain's Verses.*† NDP345.
  Residence on Earth.† NDP340.
New Directions in Prose & Poetry (Anthology).
  Available from #50 forward to #54.
Robert Nichols, *Arrival.* NDP437.
  Exile. NDP485. *Garh City.* NDP450.
  Harditts in Sawna. NDP470.
J. F. Nims, *The Six-Cornered Snowflake.* NDP700.
Charles Olson, *Selected Writings.* NDP231.
Toby Olson, *The Life of Jesus.* NDP417.
  Seaview. NDP532.
George Oppen, *Collected Poems.* NDP418.
István Örkeny, *The Flower Show / The Toth Family.*
  NDP536.
Wilfred Owen, *Collected Poems.* NDP210.
José Emilio Pacheco, *Battles in the Desert.* NDP637.
  Selected Poems.† NDP638.
Nicanor Parra, *Antipoems: New & Selected.* NDP603.
Boris Pasternak, *Safe Conduct.* NDP77.
Kenneth Patchen, *Aflame and Afun.* NDP292.
  Because It Is. NDP83.
  Collected Poems. NDP284.
  Selected Poems. NDP160.
Octavio Paz, *Configurations.*† NDP303.
  A Draft of Shadows.† NDP489.
  Eagle or Sun?† NDP422.
  Selected Poems. NDP574.
  A Tree Within.† NDP661.
St. John Perse, *Selected Poems.*† NDP545.
J. A. Porter, *Eelgrass.* NDP438.
Ezra Pound, *ABC of Reading.* NDP89.
  Confucius. NDP285.
  Confucius to Cummings. (Anth.) NDP126.
  A Draft of XXX Cantos. NDP690.
  Elektra. NDP683.
  Gaudier Brzeska. NDP372.
  Guide to Kulchur. NDP257.
  Literary Essays. NDP250.
  Selected Cantos. NDP304.
  Selected Letters 1907-1941. NDP317.
  Selected Poems. NDP66.
  The Spirit of Romance. NDP266.
  Translations.† (Enlarged Edition) NDP145.
Raymond Queneau, *The Blue Flowers.* NDP595.
  Exercises in Style. NDP513.
  The Flight of Icarus. NDP358.
Mary de Rachewiltz, *Ezra Pound.* NDP405.
Raja Rao, *Kanthapura.* NDP224.
Herbert Read, *The Green Child.* NDP208.
P. Reverdy, *Selected Poems.*† NDP346.
Kenneth Rexroth, *Classics Revisited.* NDP621.
  More Classics Revisited. NDP668.
  100 More Poems from the Chinese. NDP308.
  100 More Poems from the Japanese.† NDP420.
  100 Poems from the Chinese. NDP192.
  100 Poems from the Japanese.† NDP147.
  Selected Poems. NDP581.
  Women Poets of China. NDP528.
  Women Poets of Japan. NDP527.
  World Outside the Window, Sel. Essays. NDP639.
Rainer Maria Rilke, *Poems from The Book of Hours.*
  NDP408.
  Possibility of Being. (Poems). NDP436.
  Where Silence Reigns. (Prose). NDP464.
Arthur Rimbaud, *Illuminations.*† NDP56.
  Season in Hell & Drunken Boat.† NDP97.
Edouard Roditi, *Delights of Turkey.* NDP445.
  Oscar Wilde. NDP624.
Jerome Rothenberg, *Khurbn.* NDP679.
  New Selected Poems. NDP625.
Nayantara Sahgal, *Rich Like Us.* NDP665.

Ihara Saikaku, *The Life of an Amorous Woman.*
  NDP270.
St. John of the Cross, *Poems.*† NDP341.
William Saroyan, *Madness in the Family.* NDP691.
Jean-Paul Sartre, *Nausea.* NDP82.
  The Wall (Intimacy). NDP272.
Peter Dale Scott, *Coming to Jakarta.* NDP672.
Delmore Schwartz, *Selected Poems.* NDP241.
  The Ego Is Always at the Wheel. NDP641.
  In Dreams Begin Responsibilities. NDP454.
  Last & Lost Poems. NDP673.
Shattan, *Manimekhalai.* NDP674.
Stevie Smith, *Collected Poems.* NDP562.
  New Selected Poems. NDP659.
  Some Are More Human. . . . NDP680.
Gary Snyder, *The Back Country.* NDP249.
  The Real Work. NDP499.
  Regarding Wave. NDP306.
  Turtle Island. NDP381.
G. Sobin, *Voyaging Portraits.* NDP651.
Enid Starkie, *Rimbaud.* NDP254.
Robert Steiner, *Bathers.* NDP495.
Antonio Tabucchi, *Letter from Casablanca.* NDP620.
  Little Misunderstandings. . . . NDP681.
Dylan Thomas, *Adventures in the Skin Trade.* NDP183.
  A Child's Christmas in Wales. NDP181.
  Collected Poems 1934-1952. NDP316.
  Collected Stories. NDP626.
  Portrait of the Artist as a Young Dog. NDP51.
  Quite Early One Morning. NDP90.
  Under Milk Wood. NDP73.
Tian Wen: *A Chinese Book of Origins.* NDP624.
Uwe Timm, *The Snake Tree.* NDP686.
Niccolo Tucci, *The Rain Came Last.* NDP688.
Tu Fu, *Selected Poems.* NDP675.
Lionel Trilling, *E. M. Forster.* NDP189.
Martin Turnell, *Baudelaire.* NDP336.
Paul Valéry, *Selected Writings.*† NDP184.
Elio Vittorini, *A Vittorini Omnibus.* NDP366.
Rosmarie Waldrop, *The Reproduction of Profiles.*
  NDP649.
Robert Penn Warren, *At Heaven's Gate.* NDP588.
Vernon Watkins, *Selected Poems.* NDP221.
Eliot Weinberger, *Works on Paper.* NDP627.
Nathanael West, *Miss Lonelyhearts & Day of the Locust.*
  NDP125.
J. Wheelwright, *Collected Poems.* NDP544.
Tennessee Williams, *Camino Real.* NDP301.
  Cat on a Hot Tin Roof. NDP398.
  Clothes for a Summer Hotel. NDP556.
  The Glass Menagerie. NDP218.
  Hard Candy. NDP225.
  In the Winter of Cities. NDP154.
  A Lovely Sunday for Creve Coeur. NDP497.
  One Arm & Other Stories. NDP237.
  Red Devil Battery Sign. NDP650.
  A Streetcar Named Desire. NDP501.
  Sweet Bird of Youth. NDP409.
  Twenty-Seven Wagons Full of Cotton. NDP217.
  Vieux Carre. NDP482.
William Carlos Williams,
  The Autobiography. NDP223.
  The Buildup. NDP259.
  The Doctor Stories. NDP585.
  Imaginations. NDP329.
  In the American Grain. NDP53.
  In the Money. NDP240.
  Paterson. Complete. NDP152.
  Pictures from Brueghel. NDP118.
  Selected Poems (new ed.). NDP602.
  White Mule. NDP226.
  Yes, Mrs. Williams. NDP534.
Yvor Winters, *E. A. Robinson.* NDP326.
Wisdom Books: *Early Buddhists.* NDP444; *Spanish
  Mystics.* NDP442; *St. Francis.* NDP477; *Taoists.*
  NDP509; *Wisdom of the Desert.* NDP295; *Zen
  Masters.* NDP415.

For complete listing request free catalog from
New Directions, 80 Eighth Avenue, New York 10011

†Bilingual